D1591649

The Helicopter

THE

South Brunswick and New York: A. S. Barnes and Company
London: Thomas Yoseloff Ltd

HELICOPTER

Hollingsworth Franklin Gregory
Brigadier General USAF (Ret)

© 1976 by A. S. Barnes and Co., Inc.

A. S. Barnes and Co., Inc.
Cranbury, New Jersey 08512

Thomas Yoseloff Ltd
108 New Bond Street
London W1Y OQX, England

Library of Congress Cataloging in Publication Data

Gregory, Hollingsworth Franklin, 1906–
    The helicopter.

    Published in 1944 under title: Anything a horse can do:
the story of the helicopter.
    Includes index.
    1. Helicopters. I. Title.
TL716.G68 1975   629.133′35   74-30720
ISBN 0-498-01670-6

Printed in the United States of America

To My Wife
Sarah Elizabeth Kohr Gregory

Contents

1
Da Vinci to De Bothezat

MAN HAS FLOWN high and far and fast. In the airplane he has crossed the oceans, spanned the continents, and encircled the globe. He has approached the speed of sound; indeed, surpassed it. He has invaded the cold, lonely realm of the stratosphere. Using the potentialities of a mighty air force he is winning a war that will decide the destiny of all the peoples on this earth. Now he wants one more thing from the flying machine—to individualize it, to give practically everyone the opportunity to share in the Age of Flight that is just ahead. The realization of that desire has its seed in the development of the helicopter.

Vertical flight, the basic feature of the helicopter's operation, is older than aviation itself, for man first thought of straight-up-and-down lift devices before he thought of the glider or the power-driven flying machine.

One legend goes as far back as 3000 B.C., when a Persian monarch summoned his slaves to build for him a chariot and harness to it domestically trained eagles whose powerful muscles, he thought, would lift the machine into the sky and whisk him among the clouds. Practical thinking on the subject, however, dates back to the screw principle initiated by Archimedes—man's belief that he could screw himself into the air as a ship's propeller does in the water. This theory brought about the first written words on the problem of vertical flight and led to drawings and sketches for the first helicopter, a crude, impracticable affair.

Leonardo da Vinci, the famous Italian artist, was also a poet, mathematician and scientist. He was the first to discover the secret of controlled flight when he saw what others failed to see, that birds maintained their balance by manipulating the tips of their wings. That principle was rediscovered and put into practical application by the Wright brothers centuries later. Probably more than anything else it led to the Wrights' success with their kites and the heavier-than-air flying machine. Perhaps it was da Vinci's knowledge which he learned from the flight of the birds that led him to create and set forth his ideas for a practical flying machine. That device was in principle a helicopter.

In his own words he described it: "I say that this instrument made with a helix and is well made, that is to say, of flaxen linen of which one has closed the pores with starch, and is turned with a great speed, the said helix is able to make a screw in the air and to climb high."

He had outlined a machine for flight. Moreover, he had made use of the Greek word *helix* (meaning *spiral* or *twist*,) applying it to the thought of flying. This later led to its combination with the word *pteron* (meaning *wing*) and the popular term "helicopter."

Some claim that da Vinci built models of his strange design and that these models actually were flown. One historian has recorded: "The da Vinci machines made on the helicopter principle were of paper and wire, and actuated motion by steel springs, which caused them to lift into the air." There is no authentic proof of this, but it is within reason to believe that a man of da Vinci's capabilities might have been inclined to build small models from the sketches he had conceived, merely to prove his theories. There is today a da Vinci helicopter model in the New York Museum of Science and Industry which was built by modern engineers from da Vinci's drawings. This model has never flown and appears definitely not to possess the characteristics necessary for flight. It does present one thing clearly: da Vinci's thinking was sound, though the method, shape, and structure were impracticable.

In 1868, a French engineer named Paucton, utilizing no more knowledge than da Vinci could have told him, made plans for his "Pterophore," a machine which had two turning mills, one to support the device and one to drive it along in the air. His craft was never built. It was to be operated, the inventor explained: "By means of a crank to give the Pterophore a suitable circular speed which would lift the machine vertically, but in order to move horizontally a tail in the shape of another Pterophore would supply the motion. A system of valves fixed across the end of the space between the blades automatically closes the openings through which the air flows and thus changes the Pterophore into an unbroken surface which resists the flow of air and retards the fall of the machine to a considerable degree."

About the same time, two of Paucton's countrymen, Launoy, a naturalist, and Bienvenu, an expert mechanician, developed a strange top affair embracing the principle of two air screws revolving in opposite directions. It was evident that they got their idea from a "Chinese top" mentioned in Oriental literature—which, incidentally, was probably the first device, though it was but a toy, actually to fly. They demonstrated the idea before the

First model of Breguet helicopter—first to fly with pilot aboard.

French Academy of Sciences, and thereby stemmed a great public curiosity in the machine's unusual flight antics.

One of those interested in the toy's peculiarities was an Englishman, Sir George Cayley, who listened to many of his friends describe the device when they came to visit him on his Yorkshire estate. He built a toy along the same lines, employing the basic idea but using modifications of his own design. According to his own notes, one of these toys "rose as high as ninety feet in the air." He later built gliders and flew them and once even dared approach his gardener with the insane idea that he (the gardener) ride in one of the machines. Because of his undying efforts and his research in the face of sarcastic critics who said he was "crazy as a tightrope walker," Sir George earned the title: "Father of British Aeronautics." For our purposes, he gave to the world, in one of his better moments of creativeness, plans for the first full-sized, man-carrying helicopter—a machine which got its power from a steam-driven engine and which, paradoxically enough, was not too unlike, in its design, the present-day Focke-Wulf helicopter. The idea never did get beyond the model stage, probably because the power was not available in the right form. Cayley's model had a nose shaped like a bird's beak and its body was streamlined like that of a gull. It employed a series of eight-bladed rotors for lift and two four-bladed propellers for forward motion.

Cayley's experiments were known far and wide. An Italian civil-engineering professor, Enrico Forlanini, saw in the Englishman's mention of a steam-driven helicopter an idea which he enlarged upon with a degree of success. In 1878 he succeeded in building a small model with two superimposed screws, driven by a one-quarter-horsepower steam engine. The model weighed only eight pounds and in trials lifted itself up to the astounding height of forty feet and remained there for periods up to a third of a minute. Forlanini's device, next to the Chinese top, ranks among the first of the helicopter models to achieve flight.

Prior to this, an American, William C. Powers, had advanced ideas for an invention to be used as a "bomber" employing the principles of a helicopter. Powers was a captain in the Confederate Army and his "bomber" was intended to break the Union blockade of the Southern ports. He also claimed it to be an excellent machine for observation and reconnaissance and of great military value. It consisted of a series of air screws both vertical and horizontal, apparently to give it lift and forward motion. A picture of the device, uncovered years later, looked more like a new-type plow than anything else, but descriptive data indicated that Powers meant it to be a machine for flight. It most certainly would never have flown. The officer abandoned the idea because he was afraid it might get into the hands of Union soldiers and boomerang against the boys in gray.

There were many experimenters who followed in the design steps of Forlanini and Cayley. These included Kress, a German; Wellner, an Austrian, and W. R. Kimball, an American. None of these made any worth-while improvements in the ideas that had gone before them. They did one thing important to the helicopter: they kept the idea alive.

Gustav Trouve, whose explosive-powered ornithopter created a sensation, built an electrically powered helicopter in 1887. A small electric motor of remarkably light weight enabled the model to fly successfully. The current was obtained through a pair of thin trailing wires. Trouve then sought to build a larger, full-scale helicopter and proposed that it would be "of great value for military uses such as observation and reconnaissance."

The idea of electric power for flying machines fascinated American inventors, including the great Thomas A. Edison. That this American genius was seeking to explore the field is revealed in one of his biographies, which quotes the inventor as saying: "James Gordon Bennett came to me and asked that I try some primary experiments to see if aerial navigation were feasible with heavier-than-air machines. I got up a motor and put it on the scales and tried a number of different things and contrivances connected to the motor to see how it would lighten itself on the scale. I got some data and made up my mind that what was needed was a very powerful engine for its weight. So I conceived of an engine employing guncotton. I took a lot of ticker tape, turned it into guncotton, and got up an engine with an arrangement whereby I could feed this guncotton strip into the cylinder and explode it inside electrically. The feed took place between two copper rolls. The copper kept the temperature down as the strip was in contact with the feed rolls. It worked pretty well; but one machine roll didn't take it and the flame went through and exploded the whole roll and kicked up such an explosion that I abandoned it. But the idea might be made to work." That Edison, if he had obtained the motivation from his exploding motor, would have turned to the principle of vertical flight is illustrated convincingly by this statement he made years after the experiment: "Whatever progress the airplane might make, the helicopter will come to be taken up by the advanced students of aeronautics."

Another famous American inventor, Emile Berliner, who had to his credit the development of the gramophone and many other now commonplace devices, thought too of the helicopter. An ardent follower of the Wright brothers, he believed, nevertheless, that these two experimenters were going about their efforts in the wrong way. "The way to fly," he once wrote a friend, "is to go straight up." He was certainly thinking of the helicopter.

J. Newton Williams, another American, worked with him on his ideas. Williams had gained considerable experience in aeronautics while working with Glenn Curtiss at Hammondsport and Curtiss was the second authority in America on the airplane; later he built some of the best machines this country ever owned. Berliner and Williams built a craft in 1908-09, but an unfortunate accident destroyed it.

Berliner's thoughts about the Wrights were a bit inaccurate. Wilbur and Orville Wright both were familiar with the helicopter principle since their childhood, when their father, the Bishop Milton Wright, brought home for the boys to play with a toy helicopter top, a replica of the top that Launoy and Bienvenu had introduced in France. During my last visit with Orville Wright he asserted: "We made many of these small toys, fashioning the blades of bamboo and tissue paper, and we flew them with great success. But we learned early that the bigger the blades were, the worse they would react in the air. We had these toys in 1878. I can't say that our thought was influenced by them. We thought the helicopter more difficult: consequently, when we turned to the development of the flying machine our favoritism was towards the glider methods of Chanute and Lilienthal."

The famous inventor, who will be seventy-three years old this year, now foresees possibilities for the helicopter. "Such a machine," he predicts, "will never compete with the airplane, though it will have specialized uses, and in these it will surpass the airplane. The fact that you can land at your front door is the reason you can't carry heavy loads efficiently."

Helicopter designed and built by Paul Cornu.

At the turn of the century the stage was set. The idea had advanced. Models had flown successfully. Full-sized, man-carrying helicopters had been sketched, planned, and talked about. It remained for someone to build the full-scale machine. That honor went to a French engineer, Louis Breguet, who, it is claimed, on August 24, 1907, nearly four years after the conventional airplane had flown at Kittyhawk, flew his machine, the first helicopter to leave the ground with a pilot aboard. The Breguet craft had four lifting air screws, which made it one of the first of the early designs to have four-point suspension. Each of the air screws consisted of four large biplane blades.

In the air the craft, having no means of control, was highly unstable, but its inventor learned from it that it was possible to leave the ground by using rotating wings. He built his second helicopter in the winter of 1907-08 and incorporated ideas which proved impracticable for controlling the machine. The following year he built another machine, but achieved little further success, and for that reason Breguet temporarily dropped his experiments with vertical flight.

The first man to fly in a helicopter did not, however, give up aviation. He continued with other designs along the lines of the more conventional airplane and succeeded in becoming one of the outstanding French airplane designers. His airplanes have been known the world over.

Shortly after the first flights by Breguet one of his countrymen, Paul Cornu, built a full-scale helicopter which showed some promise of actually flying. This machine was an approach to modern designs. It was a twin-rotor affair. The rotors were twenty feet in diameter, mounted on outriggers, and longitudinally disposed. The craft was driven by an Antoinette airplane engine developing 24 horsepower. The motor virtually rested in the pilot's lap. Four bicycle wheels supported the contraption, the structure of which was a scanty framework. Allegedly it got into the air in some of its trials, but only for a few feet, and it remained sustained there only for about twenty-second periods. There was little, if any, controllability. That its control was poor was a factor that need not have discouraged its inventor. This factor, probably more than any other, held back vertical-flight successes for years.

In the year 1909, a young, ambitious Russian aeronautical enthusiast, Igor Sikorsky, visited Paris, which at that time was agog at the astonishing exhibitions of flying done by Wilbur Wright, the American aviator, who had built and flown the first successful heavier-than-air flying machine. Everywhere Sikorsky went, Frenchmen told him of the older Wright brother and his daring flights. The young man, already a follower of the Wrights, turned to the serious side of aviation and decided to build a flying machine of his own design. Despite the success of the Wright brothers and because of his own individualistic thinking, he turned to the idea of the helicopter. Firstly, he needed power. He found this in a French Anzani motor, 25 horsepower, three cylinders, which had been used successfully in a number of

French-built airplanes. Secondly, he needed money. His sister, Olga, supplied the finances on a family loan basis. Then Sikorsky went to work on the design. It didn't prove to be much. The craft had two concentric lifting propellers or rotors. They were mounted one above the other. One was sixteen and a half feet in diameter; the smaller one, an even sixteen feet across. These were rotated in opposite directions at approximately 160 revolutions per minute, enough to create a good lifting force. By the summer of 1909—about the same time the Army tested and accepted its first airplane from the Wrights at Fort Meyer, Virginia, the first military airplane in the world—Sikorsky was ready to fly his helicopter. It was the forerunner of another machine that he was to sell years later to the same Army, another first in the world's annals of aviation.

The first Sikorsky helicopter looked ground-bound. It was quite apparent to those who saw it that the craft would never leave the earth. No one admitted this more readily than its inventor. When the engine was started it vibrated and shook worse than Henry Ford's first wheezing, jumping jallopy. It showed no signs of lifting itself into the air, and it didn't.

Sikorsky, undaunted, spent the following winter working over the design, changing it, improving it, and in the spring of the next year he was ready to try again. Results were better. The vibration was still there, but not to too great a degree. The ship flew. It lifted its own weight of approximately four hundred pounds. But it would lift nothing more—no passengers, no pilot. In effect, it was an overgrown model. The inventor could not remedy the situation, finally dropped the whole project, and focused his attention on the conventional airplane. He has since become distinguished as one of the world's foremost plane designers, at first as the builder of great multiengined machines for the Czar of Russia and more recently as the designer of the famous Clipper planes that have paved the way across the Pacific and the Atlantic. By 1910 Sikorsky was through with helicopters. He was to return some years later. Not too much progress was made in between.

The First World War found the airplane an infant. At the outbreak of the conflict none of the belligerents possessed many airplanes. France had a few flying machines, Germany was experimenting with various types, England and America were offering big prizes to fliers, but actually the airplane was not very far advanced. As a weapon it had been thought of, but at first the fighting armies began using it merely as a mobile observation post. German aviators made frequent reconnaissance flights over Paris. The French retaliated. There was no air fighting. The men on both sides waved to each other from their planes. There was a good-fellowship and a friendliness between the enemies, a sort of brotherhood of the sky. That grew to animosity in the early part of 1915 when the pilots started throwing bricks and spikes at each other. Then they tried guns and bullets. War in the sky began in earnest. Planes grew larger, got more guns, flew faster, carried more bombs. Meanwhile the helicopter progressed very little. It was practically forgotten except that strategists on both sides thought of a machine "that could hover in the sky over the enemy and spot his movements." They utilized the "sausage" balloons, but they really wanted a practical helicopter.

A report from the American military attaché in Paris regarding European developments during the World War period states: "The idea of building a captive helicopter was first conceived by Lieutenant Petroczy of the Austrian Army in April, 1915. His apparatus was to be equipped with a 200-horsepower motor, and the engine was ordered from the Daimler Company, which guaranteed its weight not to exceed 250 kilograms (550 pounds). Petroczy's idea was not carried out, and the realization of a captive helicopter was dealt with again by Professor Karman, a professor in aerodynamics at Aix-la-Chappelle, attached to the Technical Service of the Austrian Army during the war."

The man referred to in the attaché's report was Professor Theodore von Karman, who today is still active in aviation, Director of Aeronautical Research at the California Institute of Technology. The helicopter they built was provided with two coaxial propellers, one above the other, and revolving in opposite directions. The craft had three 120-horsepower Le Rhône engines connected to the propellers by shafts and cone gears. It weighed approximately 3200 pounds and carried, besides the pilot, one observer and a machine gun, plus enough fuel for about an hour's operation. The crew compartment was on top, above the rotors. The aircraft was never allowed to fly free, but was held captive by cables attached to the ground to stabilize it. The machine possessed no means of horizontal motivation and could not move about in the air at the pilot's will. It was a powered kite.

Tests with the Petroczy-von Karman machine were carried on for several months, during which time the helicopter performed successful ascents to an altitude of approximately fifty meters. Those who saw the tests concurred that the craft flew better when there were slight winds than it did in still air. In the course of the last test the motors did not function properly and the machine, oscillating rapidly during descent, fell off on one side, crashed, and was destroyed.

There were other attempts at the problem of vertical flight during the war. The French were interested in the Douheret helicopter, a machine composed of two horizontal propellers having the same axis. This craft did not fly, however, until 1919, and then it succeeded in lifting only its own weight.

Toussaint's helicopter was a most radical attempt, it being a craft comprising a multiplane wing system consisting of ten planes. It never flew. These are a few of the recorded attempts made from 1914-19. Other than Petroczy's and Karman's captive helicopter there was no worth-while progress made toward the practical utilization of a machine for vertical ascent, nor were there any great strides made in the period immediately following the Armistice.

The next truly great step forward came in 1922, as the result of one and a half year's work, by a Russian scientist who had come to this country a few years before and aroused considerable interest with his papers and lectures on the principles of vertical flight. Alert to take advantage of what seemed the most practical solution to the problem ever to be presented, engineers and experts of the Air Service Engineering Division gave the man the "break" for which he was waiting. The Russian inventor's name was de Bothezat.

2
The Army's First Helicopter

ARMY INTEREST in the helicopter began in 1918 just after the Armistice, when an investigation of the Peter Cooper Hewitt helicopter design was made by the Air Service Engineering Division at McCook Field. They foresaw "great possibilities" for a machine capable of up-and-down flight and hence operation from restricted areas. Consequently every effort was made on their part to study all the developments here and abroad pertaining to helicopter flight. In the following year, tests were run on a small one-quarter scale model of the J. E. McWorter "Autoplane." Primarily, efforts were directed to the de Bothezat machine.

George de Bothezat was a Russian exile. Like many of the great and learned men of Russia in the bloody years of the Bolshevik Revolution, he was forced to leave his native country. Miraculously he escaped the terror regime, turned first to Europe and then to America to air his ideas on science and mathematics, for which he had won world acclaim. He was a big, heavy-set person and he looked typically the scientist that he was—a man of temper, an individualist, keen, quick-witted, egotistical. Once he boasted publicly, "I am the world's greatest scientist and outstanding mathematician." Many doubted him. Few proved him wrong.

When he came to America his fame had reached here before him. There was little doubt that he was the world's foremost authority on vertical flight. The theories on helicopter principles —about which he had talked in lectures and on which he had written long, detailed reports—were sound, tangible, and workable. As early as 1916 he had published the first theory of lifting screws, a treatise which gave complete and exact data for designing helicopter screws. The report was published later in this country by the N.A.C.A. (National Advisory Committee for Aeronautics), the world's foremost aeronautical research institution. At that time, the aeronautical experts of America believed that this was the only report of its kind which "gave a complete description of the whole phenomenon of computing and designing lifting screws," the basic feature of the helicopter. Such outstanding recognition of his ability placed de Bothezat at the head of the list of inventors and authorities on the helicopter.

McCook Field was the center of all U. S. military aviation, the birthplace of American air power. It was the home of the Engineering Division of the Air Service, established by Act of Congress and War Department Appropriation in 1917 for the purpose of research and experimentation in military aeronautics and the development of the flying machine. It was the first institution of its kind in the country, and the largest in the world. The men who made up its personnel were the foremost engineering authorities in aviation. Theirs was the job to design, develop, and deliver to the United States Army Air Service the best planes that man could build. They left no stone unturned in that direction, investigating thoroughly every possible invention and new idea pertaining to the advancement of the airplane. It goes without saying that they were wide-awake to helicopter development.

Many of McCook's engineers had enthusiastically read de Bothezat's theories. One such man was Major T. H. Bane, Chief of the Engineering Division in 1920, who initiated official recognition of the Russian inventor's helicopter ideas. Bane believed sincerely and wrote to his superiors that "the Air Service should undertake some positive steps toward the solution of some of the very difficult problems associated with helicopter development." He pointed out forcibly that the United States was the only great power in the world not engaged in constructive experimentation with rotary-wing aircraft and the helicopter principle of flight. Somehow we had been neglectful, perhaps chiefly because there had been so many near-successes, so many disappointments in the early tests. His engineers, explained Major Bane, had talked with every authority on the subject in this country, had labored long to work out designs and operating principles, but nowhere had they found any indications of success. Admittedly he turned to de Bothezat because the scientist had advanced ideas that seemed practicable.

Bane knew, his own engineering ability and knowledge told him, that the chief problem confronting successful helicopter flight was that of propeller blades. At least, this was the opinion he voiced more than once at closed-session meetings and in his reports. Since de Bothezat's greatest contribution to the science of aeronautics was his theory and practical demonstration of

Pilot aboard Cornu helicopter.

propeller designs, it was logical that the Chief of the Engineering Division should turn to him for help. He wrote to the Russian scientist, asked his help and advice, and later met the distinguished inventor and discussed thoroughly the whole helicopter picture. He came away convinced that the peculiar and personal knowledge of de Bothezat was the most valuable he had known. Almost immediately he began negotiations with his superior, Major General Mason Patrick, Chief of the U. S. Air Service, for permission to enter into a contract with de Bothezat for the construction of a helicopter at McCook Field. Bane was convinced that de Bothezat was so "far out ahead of anyone else with his idea" that there was no need for any open bidding for the contract and that to secure competition was impracticable.

During this period of negotiation Bane had many meetings with de Bothezat, who had come to Dayton so that he would be in close contact with the McCook Field engineers and their problems. On May 31, 1921, the Russian scientist proposed in a letter to Major Bane his solution of the helicopter problem.

An excerpt from Professor de Bothezat's letter to the Major, written in the inventor's own longhand, said: "Here will be found the complete disclosure of the helicopter invented by Prof. Dr. George de Bothezat at the end of 1917 at that time in Petrograd. It is only the special conditions created by the outbreak of the Russian Revolution that have prevented the author to realize his invention until now. The helicopter here disclosed is to the best of the author's knowledge the first to possess all qualities of complete *inherent stability* and *maneuverability* which are essential for the navigation of any vehicle of locomotion. For the simplicity of the description the main principles and features of the de Bothezat helicopters will be here described having in mind a helicopter of the following type: the helicopter considered is essentially composed of four lifting blade-screws identi-

cal in size and shape and disposed cross-wise. . . ."

The letter went on for eighteen pages, describing in detail the principles of operation and the structure of the craft de Bothezat had in mind. It was accompanied by drawings and diagrams that illustrated the various operational functions. Bane knew, and so did his associates, that this was the best and most complete functional report on helicopter operation ever written. No doubt the letter was the deciding factor in causing the Air Service to contract with de Bothezat to build the first Army helicopter.

The contract was dated June 1, 1921, a month after the inventor had written his descriptive letter to Major Bane, and it concluded long debates and discussions on the subject. At last we were going to do something about it. Both parties were pleased. By its terms de Bothezat agreed to furnish drawings and data, to design, construct, and supervise flight tests of a helicopter. The government was to furnish supplies, materials, equipment, workmen, and construction space. There were many unusual conditions; as compensation the inventor was to get $5000 for the complete first drawings and sketches. He was to receive $4800 more for the detail design and construction and $2500 additional if the machine would rise from the ground on its own power. If it should rise three hundred feet and return safely with a descending speed of less than fifteen feet per second—about ten miles per hour—with the engine completely throttled, he would get an additional $7500. Altogether by its terms the contract involved more than $19,800, to be the inventor's if his helicopter were successful. Of course, fame and fortune were awaiting him besides. There was a time limit. The government wanted the job done by January 1, 1922. It later extended the deadline to May 31, 1922, which, oddly enough, was a year to the day of the date of de Bothezat's letter to Bane. The inventor also granted to the government the license under any developments which were de-

4
Here It Is, Fly It

FORT SILL, Oklahoma, stretches out over the South-western plains of the Sooner State like a great Indian reservation. Daily thousands upon thousands of young red-blooded Americans pass through its gates to learn to be artillerymen in the United States Army. Today it is one of the busiest big training centers in all the world, turning out the fightingest men on earth. In 1932 it was one of the largest military posts in the U. S., but it was quieter then. The guns boomed loud and not infrequently across the big ranges. Instead of tens of thousands there were about five thousand soldiers and officers, permanent party, who manned the guns, ran the warehouses, staffed the Army's Field Artillery School. Two miles from the main post was Post Field. Stationed there was a flight of the 16th Observation Squadron, U. S. Army Air Corps. Flight "E" of that organization was my outfit.

Eager, ambitious, rarin' to go, just like so many other young second lieutenants whose wings were still none too strong, I was a pursuit pilot. Being assigned to an Observation Squadron wasn't exactly to my liking. The two-place, squatty-looking, old, Thomas Morse o-19's, with their corrugated fuselages and fabric-covered wings, were a far cry from the fast, sleek, taper-winged Curtiss Hawk pursuits (the P-1's) which we used to snap around the sky like a crack-the-whip at a carnival. The old Morse bi-planes were too slow. Besides, who wanted to be an observation pilot, anyhow? Didn't the observers in the last war get tagged "half-lunged roosters"? That would be pretty for a fighter pilot, wouldn't it?

I was wrong. Fort Sill for the next four years proved most enjoyable. There were the club, the tennis courts, the golf course, the friends I made, officers, enlisted men and civilians—all a part of this old airfield which was getting some much-needed new construction. My duties as Engineering Officer covered a multitude of sins and kept me busier than a bee in a tar bucket. But what I liked most was the freedom to fly, to get into the sky. There was a lot of that at Post Field in those days.

An artillery battalion owns the big guns, keeps them ready for action, cleans them, wheels them into position, feeds them the charges, fires them, blasts the enemy from his trenches or hide-outs. To be effective it must have *spotters*, men who can "see" the enemy, chart his positions, estimate the range, the angle of aim, the direction of the wind, the height of a hill or the depth of a ditch—trained experts, who are the eyes of the big guns. The last war proved that the best "spotters" were the men who could get in the highest, safest position. That gave birth to the idea of the airplane as a flying observation post, which in turn created our observation squadron. That was the reason we were at Fort Sill—to serve as the eyes for the artillery.

Our job was purely tactical. Sometimes from dawn to dusk we were in the air on sham battle missions. The old o-19's lumbered into the sky and roared over the prairie where once the wagon schooners had rumbled. We made reconnaissance flights with photographers in the rear cockpit who mapped routes and areas by the hundreds of square miles. We remained for hours in the sky over targets set up far away from the guns and directed the gunner's aim by radio telephone. Often we would fly fast and low to the ground and by an ingenious method pick up messages, then speed to a distant post and swoop low again to drop them to another battery commander. We also made short transportation hops, getting key personnel from one section to another. It was a game, but an all-serious one. We were training men for a job they had to do on a much bigger scale in the not-distant future—indeed, schooling them in the air-ground co-operation measures which have proved so decisively important in our war today.

The o-19's did the job, but they had their faults, too many of them. The struts and the wings got in the way when photographers tried to point their lenses over the side at ground objectives. The airplanes were too fast for hovering over one spot and we had to keep them at too high a speed for this work to be done effectively, primarily because that forward motion—the rush of air over their wings—was what kept them in the sky. When we skimmed low over the ground in pickups and deliveries we were taking our lives in our hands, since at that altitude any airplane is dangerous. When we made short passenger-carrying trips there was always the problem of finding a large field in which to land and from which to get out again. These factors convinced me and the others who were my associates that a better type of aircraft was needed to do this work, a unique aircraft that was slow in flight, that could hover in the air like a balloon, that could get into and out of inaccessible places which might be the hiding spot for an artillery battery. Such a craft was the helicopter.

The Pescara helicopter flies.

I had read some history of the helicopter development. It was apparent that from 1932 to 1936 there was no successful design and the future looked very dark for the possibility and realization of straight-up-and-down flight. Yet, it is important to point out that some of us, particularly the men of the Air Corps who were with the observation squadrons and therefore could understand better the need for this type of work, were thinking about rotary-winged aircraft as a possible solution to the whole problem of Army co-operation and liaison operations. My own interest in the subject was none too great, however, and other than kick the old o-19's for the job they tried to do, but didn't, I can lay no personal claim to any forward step in the right direction.

The Army had other ideas. They were going to make me take a vivid interest in the subject. I had nothing to say about it the day the orders came to report to Langley Field, Virginia, for duty with the NACA (National Advisory Committee of Aeronautics) Langley Memorial Aeronautical Laboratory.

In 1915 Congress passed an Act which created the NACA and appropriated funds to be used for "the scientific study of the problems of flight." The Langley Memorial Aeronautical Laboratory was named in honor of Professor Pierpont Langley, who came near being first to fly, but failed. In its research laboratories NACA experimenters and researchers were to delve into the unknowns of flight. They studied every new type of aircraft, the shape of its wings, its power plant, its controls and construction. In great wind tunnels they studied the effects of airflow over wing sections and propeller blades. Scarcely an airplane existed which had not been investigated here from A to Z. This was the task of NACA engineers. So that a complete and detailed study of their characteristics could be made, the Army, in the first months of 1936, sent to the NACA laboratories the two gyroplanes, YG-1 and YG-2, which it had just purchased. Two Army pilots were needed to fly them. One pilot was Lieutenant Erickson Snowden Nichols, brother of Ruth Nichols, the famous woman aviator. I was the other selected, probably because of the experience with the observation unit. It was clear to everyone, if the Autogiro was to be useful at all, it would be as a reconnaissance machine.

Views of the Pescara helicopter.

Pescara helicopter being taken from shed.

Side view of Pescara helicopter. Note warped position of wing surfaces.

Fuselage of Pescara helicopter showing Lambin radiator in tail.

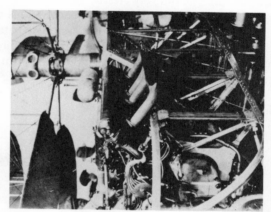

180 HP Hispano-Suiza engine used in Pescara helicopter.

Pescara flying back into courtyard after second test.

Start of Pescara helicopter on flight of 186 feet.

I met Lieutenant Nichols in the officers' bar at Langley Field the day I arrived there. I told him of my assignment.

"I'll be damned," said Nichols. "I'm the other pilot."

"Nick" became a close friend and associate.

I had seen an Autogiro (the model with fixed wings) at the air show in Detroit, Michigan, in 1931. This was all I knew of the queer-looking rotary-winged machines.

Nick had the jump on me there. He had seen the ships in the air around Langley. "They're the darnedest flying things you ever did see," he explained. "Look just like flying windmills."

The following day we were introduced to Mr. H. J. E. Reid, chief engineer in charge of the Langley laboratories, who welcomed us to the NACA. The tall, thin-faced, bass-voiced Mr. Reid was an amiable person and gave the immediate impression of being an expert in his field. Courteous, he wanted to know about our previous assignments and without mention of the detail at NACA we got acquainted. Then he began to tell us about the Autogiro and what we could expect.

I remember one thing he did very clearly.

He took us over to the big windows which bordered his office and made a sweeping gesture with his arm. "See that patch of ground right there?" he asked. "Not very big is it? Probably not any larger than a small-sized school lawn. The Autogiro can land there. It can also take off in that space. You'll be doing that someday."

At that time it seemed a long way off.

Reid continued: "The Autogiro is a strange craft. It is a direct-control gyroplane. There are no fixed wings. The machine gets all its lift from the big rotor that rotates about a central axis. The controls are the same as those of an airplane. But instead of moving ailerons or elevators you tilt the rotor forward or backward, depending upon whether you want to go down or up. It has a tail similar to an airplane. These are just some sketchy facts you should know before you see the craft."

"Have they had any trouble with them?" Nick and I asked together.

"Yes, we've had troubles," Mr. Reid admitted. "As a matter of fact we've lost one of the ships already. Bill McAvoy, our chief test pilot and an engineer, John Wheatley, were flying the YG-2 [Pitcairn] around this vicinity just two weeks ago when the tip of one of the blades exploded due to the pressure of air within the blade ripping loose a strip of fabric. The rotor was thrown out of balance and the control stick started violent gyrations in the cockpit, beating the hands and knees of the pilot. Both pilot and passenger took to their parachutes, landing safely. The accident was most unfortunate."

We agreed. But it meant less work for Nick and me.

From Reid's office we went down to the flight-test hangar and got our first glimpse of the YG-1 (Kellett), the machine we were to fly. We met Gus Crowley, who was in charge of the flight-test hangar, and Mel Gough, the NACA test pilot who was to teach us to fly the machine.

Curtiss-Bleeker helicopter.

The two models of Pescara helicopter.

At first glance the YG-1 did not look too unconventional. It was a flash of colors in an otherwise dark corner of the hangar. The blades of the rotor were a brilliant yellow and the fuselage was a marine blue. In a way it reminded one of a carnival thrill device, something to climb into with a hot dog and a root beer and "let 'er go."

Definitely, from appearance at least, it was not fit to be an aircraft. The YG-1 Autogiro provided my first real close-up inspection of a rotary-wing aircraft which, after Mr. Reid's introductory statements, seemed destined to be just the craft the Army was seeking for its observation purposes.

The YG-1 had a conventional landing gear, two wheels forward and a small tail wheel. The engine was located in the front of the fuselage as in most conventional airplanes. The fuselage or body of the ship looked very much like that of an airplane, except that no wings were attached. There were two horizontal stabilizers, small wings, in the tail of the craft which were much the same as you would find on any airplane but for the fact that they had no elevators or flippers which give an airplane its dive and climb control. In other words, these stabilizers represented a short fixed wing. Beneath this wing were two small elliptical surfaces for fins. At the very tail of the fuselage was a small rudder.

There were two open cockpits in tandem. The pilot sat in the rear position, his passenger forward. Directly in front of the passenger's cockpit was the rotor pylon, which looked more like a smokestack than anything else. At the end of this "smokestack" was mounted a windmill affair which really was the ship's rotor upon which it depended for its lift. The rotor was comprised of three blades each twenty feet long. Actually these were long, narrow wings built of steel and wood and covered with fabric. Whirling them at sufficient speed by forward motion created a lift over their surfaces and thus gave lift to the whole machine.

The cockpit had the conventional arrangement—stick, rudder pedals, throttle, and the usual complement of instruments. The new gadgets were chiefly a trio of levers—one was a clutch handle for engaging the engine with the rotor to start it in motion, another was a brake handle for stopping the rotor, and the third consisted of a lever in the floor of the cockpit. This lever, which moved in a fore and aft direction, was called a longitudinal

Helicopter by Emile Berliner.

bungee control. It accomplished the same purpose as the elevator trim tab on an airplane—trimmed the craft so that when the hands were off the stick, the aircraft had no tendency to nose down or up.

Mel Gough was a good instructor. First, he put us both at ease by telling us that the Autogiro flew very much in the same manner as the airplane. If you wanted the nose to go up, you pulled the stick back. To go down you pushed the stick forward. For banking to the left or rolling in that direction you moved the stick to the left. If you desired to roll to the right the stick was moved in that direction. The rudder was conventional in all respects and operated on the same principle as that of the airplane.

"What's he giving us—some kid's stuff?" Nick and I were thinking.

Mel must have read it in our eyes.

"You fighter pilots shouldn't have any trouble," he remarked.

Then he proceeded to tell us what was different—the tricky, unusual features of the ship's control. The stick was connected to the hub of the windmill rotor by push-pull tubes and cables; therefore, the stick controlled the tilt of the hub of the rotor. In other words, consider the rotor blades as a plate; when you pushed the stick forward the plate tilted forward and hence the aircraft descended; when you pulled the stick back, the opposite occurred. It was quite simple. Gough explained that the Autogiro required a run on the ground similar to an ordinary airplane; that prior to take-off, however, it was necessary carefully to engage the rotor with the engine by using the handle beside you, and thus allow the engine to turn the rotor up to approximately 180 revolutions per minute. At this point the rotor was declutched from the engine, the throttle opened wide, which caused the craft to move forward and autorotated the blades, the stick pulled back, and the craft lifted off the ground. After this preliminary warm-up, Gough said, the Autogiro would run along the ground for a very short distance and fairly leap into the air, climbing at a steep angle which might normally stall a conventional-type airplane.

Finished with his brief description of the ship and its control features, Mel Gough ordered the craft wheeled out of the hangar.

"Who goes first?" he wanted to know.

We had discussed this the night before and it was decided that I would be the first one to learn to fly the strange craft. I climbed into the forward cockpit and tried hard to keep my eyes on Gough's every move to get the swing of things. He pressed the little button which kicked over the compressed-air starter that in turn started the engine. The craft began to move, at first slowly, then gaining in speed as it rolled over the ground. It seemed very strange not to be looking at a pair of wings when I glanced over the side of the fuselage. It had been flown, but how I wasn't quite sure.

The first strange feeling, and it was half an alarming one, occurred when the gears clawed in and the rotor above my head began to whirl like a big top. The blades as they swept by in revolution barely skimmed over the machine in their down-slant position. Then as they gained speed they straightened out, assumed an upsweep angle. The engine purred smoothly and there was a "swooshing" sound as the airfoils cut the air. I could hear the gears let go when Gough threw the lever which declutched the rotor, but the blades kept right on rotating with little slack in speed. The throttle was opened, the craft started moving, the rotor turned faster, yet the craft itself was not moving more than forty miles an hour. This slow speed caused me great astonishment when gracefully the ship leaped into the air. I was waiting for Gough to gain more speed, but apparently this slow take-off speed was the craft's hidden secret. Never before had I known an aircraft to get into the air so quickly and with so little effort.

From then on there was nothing new about the flight. We did

Henry Berliner in flight.

Pitcairn U.S. Army YG-2 wingless autogiro.

Kellett U.S. Army YG-1 wingless autogiro.

some banks, turns, climbed a little, dived, rolled, and generally went through all the various motions to acquaint me with the feel of the ship; then Gough let me take the controls. Much to my surprise the craft flew just like an airplane with the big exception that it flew more slowly. Actually it made me feel as though I were piloting a boat rather than an aircraft.

Coming down was something else again. The craft was no longer just like an airplane. It seemed to drop out of the sky with little or no glide. The whirling rotor, still autorotating, permitted us to glide much like an airplane, but slower and steeper. It reared back for a landing. It settled with barely a bounce and rolled to a stop within about ten feet. This, then, was its other unique characteristic. I was greatly impressed and thought of the many times at Fort Sill when the boys would have given their bar tickets for such a craft as this which could plop down in any colonel's back yard.

Gough took Nichols up for a trial spin, then came down and gave me another half-hour lesson in how to fly the Autogiro. It was more of a brief refresher to see how much I had picked up during the flight.

After this he turned to me and grinned: "This time, Lieutenant, she's all yours. Go ahead, son, fly it!"

5
The Gyroplane

THE GYROPLANE is a flying machine balanced and supported by rotating horizontal or slightly inclined planes. The basic principle by which it operates goes back to nature itself. For example, look at the tiny maple seed. Study its shape carefully. Hold it a few feet from the ground and let it drop. The seed will spin to the ground. It is autorotating. In a sense, that seed is a rotating wing. The autorotation of the Autogiro, gyroplane, or whatever you choose to call it, varies little in principle from that of the maple seed. The same is true of the Australian boomerang. It, too, is a rotating wing.

The Autogiro is a gyroplane. The word Autogiro, however, is a proprietary name. It was coined and owned by the Cierva Autogiro Co. Ltd., builders of the first successful Autogiro. The name Autogiro is to the gyroplane what the name Frigidaire is to the electrical refrigerator. In other words, all electric iceboxes are not Frigidaires; all gyroplanes are not Autogiros.

There are two types of Autogiros, the fixed-wing gyroplane and the direct-control giro. Today the fixed-wing type is practically extinct. It was only built during the early development stages of the Autogiro and then principally for the purpose of providing lateral control. March, 1933, marked the advent of the direct-control Autogiro which ushered in the era of the wingless gyroplane.

The direct-control Autogiro in appearance is similar to the fixed-wing type, except it has no fixed wings. The rotor ceases to be merely an added lift device and becomes the source of the gyroplane's whole lift. One must not confuse the Autogiro with the helicopter, as many are prone to do. It must be remembered that the gyroplane has a propeller and flies much like an airplane, except that the wings are autorotating, whereas the helicopter has its rotor driven by the engine.

The craft Mel Gough, the NACA test pilot, told me to take up and solo that day back in the spring of 1936 was a direct-control Autogiro. It was the Army's YG-1 built by Kellett.

It might be well to explain here how the two autogiros, the Kellett YG-1 and the Pitcairn YG-2, first of the gyroplanes to be purchased by the Army, got their designations. The letters and numbers applied to our aircraft are part of a planned Army Air Forces (AAF) policy. Every military aircraft is especially typed according to the mission it is to perform. For instance, a bomber is given a letter designation of B for bombardment, its mission.

Thus, we have the B-19, or the B-17, the famous Flying Fortress. The numerical designation means the model number. In the case of the B-19, then, this big bomber is the nineteenth bomber design built for the Air Forces. The same is true of pursuit planes. In the designations P-40, P-51, P-38, the P stands for pursuit, the number for the model in the series of fighter aircraft. Officially today, however, the P series airplanes are called fighters, although they maintain the Pursuit designation. Perhaps the best explanation of this is modern air war itself. Our fighters today are not "pursuing," an action of World War I planes that gave birth to the popular title pursuit plane. They are fighting, attacking, defending, springing offensive actions on every front. Therefore, the name fighter plane is more appropriate.

There are other qualifications. When the model series designation is preceded by an X or a Y, these letters respectively signify experimental types or service test aircraft. Examples are the XP-38 or the XB-29. The first refers to the experimental P-38, the twin-tailed Lockheed "Lightning" which Colonel Benjamin S. Kelsey flew across the continent in 1939. The latter is the official designation of the first experimental prototypes of the big four-engined "Superfortress," the Boeing B-29.

The next series of the same models were designated YP-38's and YB-29's, airplanes built for service testing after the experimental models had proved their worth in strenuous test programs. When the letters X and Y are dropped from the designation it indicates that the aircraft has become standard equipment. When the aircraft becomes obsolete, the type letter is preceded by the letter Z; an example is the ZB-18, an obsolete-type bomber.

In the case of the Autogiros, the Army deviated from its standard practice when it named the craft YG-1 and YG-2. In this instance the G stood for Giro, since at that time there was no specific mission in mind for the rotating-wing aircraft, although most believed its principal use would be for observation. This is brought out in the fact that the present-day latest-type Autogiros have been designated the YO-61 and the YO-60, the letter O signifying Observation types. The numbers 1 and 2 following the letters on the first Autogiros indicated they were the first and second models of this type.

Going back to that first solo in the YG-1—truthfully, I cannot say that there was much difference in flying the ship alone or flying it with a passenger as I had done just before. The Autogiro, lighter with only one person aboard, got off the ground in a much shorter run. It seemed to me that when the throttle was opened the craft fairly leaped into the air. My good friend, Lieutenant Colonel John F. Biggerstaff of Wabash, Indiana, had the best description for it: "When you give 'er the throttle," he said, "she jumps fifty feet in the air and screams like a panther."

Although the YG-1 wasn't a high-powered aircraft, I learned quickly that it would leave the ground very sharply and grab at the sky for climb. It was fun to fly it. You weren't flying an airplane. You weren't flying a helicopter. This craft was something in a category of its own. That's why we later nicknamed it "The Jeep," and with all due respect to that ground-bound, rugged little four-wheeled powerhouse of the Ground Forces, the Air Forces had the first jeep in the Autogiro. At least a few of us will accept this fact. Besides, what could you call this strange-looking windmill craft that jumped into the air and jumped back down again!

After my first solo in the YG-1, I jotted down some notes for my report. These are some of the remarks: . . . "When approaching for a landing the gliding speed was approximately forty miles an hour, very slow compared to the ordinary airplane. . . . At a point when you normally start leveling off in a conventional airplane the YG-1 simply stopped, as though hung on a hook in the sky, and sat on the ground without any forward motion at all. . . . Each time a landing was made the ship controlled beautifully. . . . Nick and I like the Autogiro. . . . The craft, indeed, has possibilities."

The early-model Autogiro was nothing more than an airplane with a high lift device in the form of a four-bladed rotor. It appeared to be a plane with a windmill on top. The engine was in the nose of the craft. Cockpits or cabins were located a few feet from the nose, as in the conventional type of ship. The wings, tail, and landing gear were all very conventional. The only strange or unusual appearance about it was the rotor. The rotor was engaged with the engine by means of clutch shaft and gear mechanisms. The rotation of the rotor was started by the engine. But prior to taking off, the clutch was disengaged and the aircraft flew in the same manner as an airplane. The rotor kept turning as a result of the forces acting on the blades. In slow flight the rotor produced practically all of the lift, as the stub wing needed the flow of air over its surfaces to develop lift. Consequently, the faster the ship was flown, the more lift the stub wing would develop, simultaneously depreciating the lift forces of the rotor. There was no control of the rotor whatsoever. It was completely on its own, its action dependent upon the air through which it moved. The controls of the early-model Autogiros were conventional airplane controls—ailerons, flippers, and rudder. These controls, quite naturally, were dependent upon a relatively high speed of air flow. Thus, at slow speeds the control was none too effective. Particularly in landing, when good control is most vital, it was not always present. This was the principal reason for the development of the direct-control Autogiro. More than any-

thing else this requirement put the stub-winged Autogiros out of existence.

The craft we were flying at Langley Field, as I have said before, was a direct-control Autogiro. This Autogiro had one feature which enabled the pilot to have positive control of the craft at all times. It relied wholly upon the rotor for its lift, on the same principle as the helicopter, except that the rotor got its rotation as a result of the aircraft being pulled through the air by the propeller rather than by direct engine power.

There were many experiences with the Autogiro. One time I got the ship out for a demonstration and, when beginning the take-off, I became aware of a frightful shaking or vibration in the rotor. Knowing that such trouble had in the past disappeared, as soon as the craft was air-borne, I took off, but in the air the shaking continued even more violently. It seemed that the rotor was trying to tear itself free of the craft. As mysteriously as the trouble came about, it stopped. That was the only time that I found anything wrong with the Autogiro. Another noteworthy flight which illustrated its effectiveness as an aircraft for getting into and out of short fields.

On this particular flight a passenger, another officer, went along for a joy ride and to take some photographs. At first we flew very low over the post and he, leaning out over the side, got some splendid pictures. (It was in the days when you could photograph anything you could see.) Definitely we were proving the Autogiro an ideal craft for photo reconnaissance, although this occasion was purely in the nature of an excursion. When my passenger had used up several rolls of film, I decided to have some fun with him and throttled the ship down to a slow glide. When the engine was idling in this state there was little noise, just the "swish, swish, swish" of a huge fan like those that don't cool the small-town department stores in the summer heat.

Then I cut the engine entirely and the propeller in front stopped straight up and down. My passenger looked back at me with a start.

"What's wrong?" he demanded.

"Forced landing, maybe," I said.

"Should I jump?" he asked.

"Not yet."

Above our heads the rotor kept up its autorotation and the craft continued its glide to earth much like an airplane. We landed on the very edge of the field and with hardly any roll. Then almost at the instant when we came to a stop, I kicked over the starter, the rotor began to move again, and we took off almost straight up.

My passenger was chagrined, but he accepted my little trick with a good-natured laugh. He was, nevertheless, impressed with the Autogiro and what it could do. In this he was not alone. Lieutenant Nichols and I felt the same way about it.

During the period that Nick and I were learning to fly the Autogiro, we met three important men who have played outstanding major roles in the development of rotary-wing aircraft: Wallace W. Kellett, President of Kellett Autogiro Company,

Richard H. Prewitt, Chief Engineer of the Kellett Company, and Lou Levy (later his name was changed to Leavitt), test pilot for Kellett. They made a special trip to the NACA to meet the Army's pilots and learn how we liked the Autogiro. Leavitt arrived at the field in another Autogiro, the Kellett KD-1 (K for Kellett and D for Direct Control), which differed only slightly from the models we were flying. It was the prototype of the YG-1 and was the model built for the Army competition of a few years before.

Leavitt, with Jim Ray, of the Pitcairn Autogiro Company, were probably the most experienced Autogiro pilots in this country. Leavitt took Nichols and me up for a ride in the KD-1 giro and explained to us some of the more intimate tricks of the gyroplane. There was no question about it: he was a master of the art. We picked up some good pointers.

Dick Prewitt, whom we called the "Daddy of this Whirligig" because he actually had designed the YG-1 and engineered it into the air, told us many interesting facts about the construction of the ship—familiarization lessons that were very valuable. Wallace Kellett naturally was interested and pleased when we told him that we thought the Autogiro might be a solution for the problem of Army co-operation such as observation and photographic reconnaissance.

"You mean," Kellett interpreted, "the Army is vitally interested?"

Unofficially we informed him: "Vitally interested. The Autogiro, from the tests that we have already run with it, seems to be a great forward step in the right direction. It is a sound indication of the possibilities for such a craft of this general design and performance."

"What is the ultimate, do you think?" Kellett asked.

Together we asserted: "A craft that can go straight up and down. The Autogiro does the job halfway. A successful helicopter would be better."

Kellett smiled: "Yes, perhaps, but we will improve."

The steady improvement of the Autogiro, more than anything else, helped to bring about the first successful helicopter. It was the practical proving ground that gave us the key to controllable vertical flight.

This was still in the spring of 1936. On May 15 of that year I received orders appointing First Lieutenant H. F. Gregory, A.C., senior officer in charge of Autogiro Tests at Langley Field. The assignment was more flexible than that. It involved taking the

Autogiro away from the NACA for co-operative tests with ground services. Specifically the orders stated: (1) In conjunction with continuing experimental and service tests of the Autogiro, you are directed to report to the Commanding Officer at Fort Bragg, N. C. (2) In conjunction with the operation of the Autogiro, you will conform to the following limitations:

a. Diving speed, power on or power off, shall not exceed 130 m.p.h.

b. No acrobatics shall be performed.

c. No slips or skids shall be made at air speeds above 80 m.p.h.

d. Weight carried in the baggage compartment shall not exceed an amount (thirty pounds) provided for as marked on the baggage compartment.

e. No pilots other than those instructed by the National Advisory Committee for Aeronautics shall be permitted to fly the Autogiro, except by express permission of the Office of the Chief of the Air Corps.

The orders further read: In regard to tests to determine the practicability and serviceability of Autogiros for co-operative missions with the Field Artillery at Fort Bragg, you will: (1) Confer with heavier-than-air and lighter-than-air unit commanders and request that all Air Corps officers stationed at that post, insofar as possible, observe the conduct of the various tests in order to be able to make comparisons of the practicability of the Autogiro as compared with the airplane and the captive balloon. (2) Careful record will be kept of every flight and mission, with results, including time required, difficulties encountered, and type of flying required. (3) Submit comments as to the advisability of the Autogiro replacing the balloon for observation purposes. (4) Submit comments as to the practicability of developing the Autogiro for other observation missions, taking into consideration its vulnerability to attack from, and limited defense against, attacking aircraft. Problems in which attacks by airplanes are simulated are considered advisable in order to estimate the range at which the Autogiro can operate with a reasonable chance of being able to escape from hostile attack.

The task ahead was, indeed, a big one. Nichols and I had flown the Autogiro at Langley for more than fifty-six hours. The NACA pilots had added another forty-nine hours to its logbooks. We were fairly familiar with the craft. We knew its capabilities. Now we were going to learn its worth as a military machine.

One question remained to be answered: Was it the right type of aircraft to solve the problem of Army co-operation?

6
Eyes for the Big Guns

OVER THE BIG Field Artillery Range at Fort Bragg, N. C., which was covered with pine and oak forest, a lone Autogiro droned in the clear blue sky. I was at the controls and Nick was the observer. Together we were carrying out a fire adjustment mission for Battery B of the 17th Field Artillery, whose guns and headquarters were set up in the woods directly below us. The target was an old shack some two thousand yards distant. The men behind the guns on the ground couldn't see the target. From our lofty perch the shack was clearly distinguishable. Our job was to get the guns on the target. Literally we were eyes for the guns.

The YG , which Nichols had flown from Langley Field to Fort Bragg a few days before, behaved splendidly, flying slowly over the Battery Commander's station. Suddenly, above the roar of the engine, we heard the boom of the gun, saw its flash and, seconds later, the puff of dirt and smoke as the shell struck in the target area.

Lieutenant Nichols, whose job as observer was to keep the battery informed of its hits, spoke into the mike: "Two zero zero over and four zero left."

The gun boomed again.

"One zero zero short, one zero right," Nick said.

A third shell flashed; a third puff.

"On target," said Nick.

"How's that?" asked the Battery Commander.

"Nice goin'," replied Nick.

Then the real fun began. The boys on the ground spotted them first and warned Nick on the radio: "Enemy aircraft approaching. Enemy aircraft. Better duck for cover." Nick in turn pointed to the west, and there they were racing down from altitude, making a pass at an attack—three pursuit planes out to get the observers who had spotted the ground target and indirectly destroyed it.

When I saw them coming we were at about a thousand feet. They were at least four times that high and coming fast. There was but one evasive action: spiral the ship to earth and keep her out of their gun sights. The Autogiro was capable of corkscrewing to the ground. I gave her fast vertical speed in sharp turns. The fighters swooped over. They didn't get us.

This was one of the sham battles we often staged at Fort Bragg with the YG-1 Autogiro to learn how effective the craft was in evading fighter attack while it was in the air on an observation mission. There was one definite conclusion, one proof of the tests: the fighters could make only one pass at the ship and then they were through. Because they didn't use real gunfire, there was, of course, no way of determining whether they would have been successful. But one thing appeared certain: most of the time we managed to keep out of their gun sights. The Autogiro proved highly maneuverable and in this characteristic we saw good possibilities for its safety against attacking fighters. There was little doubt but that the Autogiro used this way as a flying observation post was safer than the sausage balloons used in World War I days.

When the YG-1 landed at Pope Field, Fort Bragg, on May 26, 1936, we began almost immediately a long series of tests in conjunction with the Artillery there. With us, to keep the lone Autogiro in servicable condition, were two enlisted men, Corporal J. M. Teton and Private John W. Ludington, both of whom the NACA experts had schooled in the care of the rotary-winged aircraft. They were excellent crew chiefs for the craft. Never once did we have any trouble from poor maintenance.

First came the familiarization flights. We took several Field Artillery officers up on short ten-minute flights to acquaint them with this new craft. When they landed, all expressed keen interest in the Autogiro and said they believed the craft had great possibilities as an observation auxiliary for artillery.

On one flight I took Captain J. W. Benson of the Air Corps on a test for the purpose of trying out binoculars in the Autogiro. Use of powerful binoculars in an airplane is practically impossible because of the excessive vibration. But we thought there might be some practicability in their use from the Autogiro. We stayed in the air for more than a half-hour and Benson got a good eyeful of the surrounding countryside. When we landed he was enthusiastic.

"With a little practice, binoculars could be used successfully," he remarked, "but it would be better if we could get a slower craft with less vibration."

Another test was the use of radio air-to-ground communication from the YG-1. With Staff Sergeant Warren, of the Radio Section of the 16th Observation Squadron stationed at Pope Field, as a passenger, Nichols tried out the radio with the "crackle box" mounted up under the instrument panel and the antenna mast alongside the pylon. This was a disappointment, for the engine was not shielded and thus reception was limited to positions directly above the ground stations. Even then it was weak and not very intelligible. However, for a distance of about five miles, air-to-ground voice reception was fairly good. We thought the trouble lay in the location of the radio and changed this so that the set was in front of the right foot. It was difficult to reach the right rudder pedal because of the radio in its new location, but the reception was improved with a maximum distance of ten miles. Ground-to-air reception was still very poor and limited to directly above the ground station.

These attempts and failures with the radio led to a new idea. Balloonists had used the regular wire telephone for their communication with ground crews. That was one distinctive advantage of the observation balloon over the airplane. The heavier-than-air craft could only use radio with its crackling and static. The balloon could use direct wire telephone. The airplane could not. Yet we attempted a direct telephone communication system with the Autogiro and it proved successful.

Of a necessity these tests had to be made with whatever equipment was available, and that was none too good. They were strictly of the trial-and-error variety. Mostly it was guesswork and prayer. Two persons were necessary in the Autogiro to accomplish the tests, the pilot and an observer. The pilot's job was to keep the ship level and above the ground station. The observer took care of the wires and the conversation.

I was pilot of the aircraft on the first attempt, Nick the observer. When we got up to about two hundred feet he payed out over the side from a small hand spool some light latex-covered telephone wire. At its end was an ordinary plug like that which fits into a wall phone. The men on the ground had little difficulty in grabbing the trailing wire and joining it to the ground installations. There was no brake on the hand spool, however, and as

Pitcairn PA-36 Roadable autogiro.

An autogiro with wings.

I climbed the Autogiro Nick was unable to stop the wire from unwinding and consequently all the wire was pulled off.

The next try we did it a different way. A large reel of telephone wire was borrowed from the Balloon Company, two-hundred-foot loops of it were laid out on the flying field, and the wire from the Autogiro was attached to the ground wire before take-off. When the ship got off the ground and attained an altitude of about a thousand feet, there was so much inertia in the reel that the wire broke off before the reel started turning.

Attempt number three was successful.

This time I was the observer and Nick did the piloting. The Autogiro was placed directly in front of the reel of wire and the line from the ship was connected directly to the line on the reel. The craft took off, pulling the wire behind it, and climbed to two thousand feet without any difficulty. There we remained and continued at a speed of about twenty miles per hour, cruising in a very tight circle over the ground crew. After several words with the ground commander, an artillery officer, we thought, with perhaps a bit of overconfidence at our success, something big ought to come of this first air-to-ground wire telephone conversation from an airplane. The feat had never been accomplished before and only the advent of the Autogiro made it possible.

"Connect me with the post switchboard," I asked the ground crew.

Almost instantly came the familiar, "Operator."

"May I talk to the Commanding General, please."

"General McCloskey speaking."

"This is Lieutenant Gregory, sir; I'm talking to you from an Autogiro that's flying around just a mile or so from your office. We thought, sir, you'd like to be one of the first to talk by telephone to a heavier-than-air craft in flight."

"What the blankety-blank is this?" the General roared.

When I explained to him the full significance of the event, he said he was quite thrilled at the occasion and continued to talk for five minutes or more about what a strange feeling it was to look out his office windows and see an aircraft in flight and at the same time be talking to the observer in that craft by ordinary telephone.

The communication between air and ground was excellent. But we had done more than prove the telephone practicable for this purpose. The experiment also indicated the feasibility of using this type aircraft for laying wire across ravines or impenetrable swamps. The successful method with which we had set up the first aircraft telephone system indicated this could be done.

The next tests were concerned with camouflage of the Autogiro on the ground. The ship was landed in a small clearing near some woods to demonstrate the practicability of landing in a small area near concealment. The rotor blades were folded back over the tail surfaces. Four men then pushed the ship into the low scrub pine and oak growth and covered it with branches spread over an ordinary Field Artillery gun camouflage net. Later when photographs were made of the area from the air, the prints revealed that the Autogiro was completely hidden.

Ground troops have often complained that when they needed immediate aerial observation it took too long for them to get it in order to utilize it to its fullest value. It was decided, therefore, to make some ground towing tests to determine the Autogiro's roadability—to have the Autogiro go along as part of a marching column in order to be available instantly when it was needed. The Autogiro would have no difficulty, we knew, getting off the roadway or landing again in a like spot.

The Ordnance Company at Fort Bragg manufactured a device for towing the Autogiro. They got me into the craft one day and pulled it behind a towcart for five miles, steering the Autogiro by means of its tail wheel. I soon learned that the wheels were not castered properly, and considerable difficulty was encountered when we went around sharp curves. It was much easier to

fly the ship than to drive it on the ground. The whole idea worked, but it was not any too practicable. Both Nichols and I recommended that for this purpose the landing gear of the craft should be made more rugged and designed for more flexibility.

"A better idea," Nick suggested in a report, "would be to have a low underslung semitrailer such as used by commercial moving firms. The Autogiro could be pushed up on the trailer by two men, and the mechanics or crew chief, plus their spare gear, tools, and extra gas, could be carried in the cab which pulled the trailer."

Actual reports of further tests with the Autogiro during this period recorded: "Tested the possibility of visual signals using blinker-type lamp. Signals were distinguished without difficulty both ways up to 1500 feet. A flight was made for comparison of advantages and disadvantages in artillery adjustment at a range of approximately 8000 yards, from balloon and Autogiro. Adjustments were successful from both craft. One 155-mm. gun was used. Radio was received in Autogiro, reception being successful when the engine was throttled. Telephone communication used by the balloon was more successful. A flight was made for adjustment of artillery fire by heavier-than-air observation craft from vicinity of a position over the battery. Visibility was very poor, and small black shadows of clouds drifting across the field made the observation of the small bursts of black smoke from the 155-mm. shells difficult to spot. Adjustment was satisfactory from a closer range. Two adjustments were made on this flight. The second adjustment was conducted over the battery position and, although the visibility was very bad and the observation difficult, the adjustment was satisfactory."

On June 9, 1936, less than a month after the YG-1 had arrived at Fort Bragg for the tests, misfortune struck. Nick narrowly escaped injury. Private C. A. Wille of the 16th Observation Squadron, a young chap who had been helping us with the hangar work on the craft, finally got Nick to give him a ride in the craft. His came near being the last ride. Nick had made one flight around the field and landed, experiencing a moderate amount of roughness—so he paused for a moment, then attempted a take-off. Just before he was ready to go into the air the rotor developed serious vibrations and he stopped to allow the shaking to stop. It was nothing unusual, having occurred several times previously both with Nick and when I was flying the machine. But this time it was different. It stopped for a moment, then when he gunned the engine for take-off, the virbrations were renewed with terrific force. The YG-1 began to do a ground jig, jumping up and down on its wheels like a prancing horse. This strain on the wheels severed the left landing strut, dropping the craft so that one of the rotor blades was cut off by the propeller and the others churned into the ground, ripping themselves to shreds. The short blade swooshed low over the cockpit and hit the headrest just in back of the pilot, narrowly missing Nick's neck. The pylon was torn loose and the fuselage was slightly damaged where one blade struck the tail. Although it was not beyond repair, the YG-1 was due for the hospital.

Focke Achgelis FW-61.

Thankful that he got out without a scratch, Private Wille disgustedly told Nick: "Gosh dangit, Lieutenant, I guess I won't be able to ride in it again for a while."

Nichols was equally disgusted.

He was just crawling out of the wreckage as I drove out onto the field and saw the Autogiro in its wrangled heap. When I got within calling distance of him he was shouting: "Frank, I guess there still are a couple things we don't know about this thingumajig."

He was perfectly correct. There were a lot of things we had to learn and the best way to acquire some of the knowledge, I believed, was to go to the Kellett Autogiro Corporation in Philadelphia and watch them rebuild the YG-1. This we did and we were also impressed with the new YG-1A under construction. That job was completed in little more than two months, including the two weeks it took the aircraft to make the trip in a freight car. We accepted delivery of the repaired Autogiro at 4 P.M. on August 18, 1936, and prepared to return to Fort Bragg for further tests. Nichols again was the ferry pilot, for he was what he called a "glutton for the rotors, they're so nice and slow and lazy." This time he stopped at Fort Monroe to demonstrate the Autogiro to a group of Coast Artillery officers. There was a week's delay there to repair some radio trouble and then he proceeded again to Fort Bragg, where the Artillery Board Officers outlined a rigid test program that was to last one full month.

Here are some of the further tests: At request of the Field Artillery Board, Lieutenant Nichols acted as observer and conducted the adjustment of a battery of 4.7-inch guns at their midrange, or a distance of about 7000 yards. The adjustment was made from the Autogiro. The airplane and the balloon conducted an adjustment at the same time on the same problem, for purpose of comparison. All three types of aircraft were restricted to flying no closer to the target than the battery position. The battery followed the adjustment of the airplane, although the recommendations from the Autogiro were very satisfactory.

Captain D. P. Poteet, Field Artillery Officer, was my passenger on a night reconnaissance mission for the purpose of determining the possibility of locating targets on a dark night without a moon. The night was clear and it was found easier to locate targets by starlight than on nights when the sky was overcast. Interdiction targets such as roads and road junctions were easily located.

Nichols, with Lieutenant E. H. Rice as an observer, conducted from the Autogiro the adjustment of a battery of 4.7 guns at their long range, or a distance of over 9200 yards. The airplane and the balloon conducted an adjustment at the same time on the same target, for the purpose of comparison. The battery followed the adjustment of the Autogiro. Another target was then located by the observer in the Autogiro, who reported its location by coordinates and adjusted fire on it by a shift from the previous target. Excellent adjustments were obtained in both cases from the Autogiro.

Both Nick and I conducted a night adjustment of 4.7-inch guns at their long range (9200 yards). The target consisted of crossroads to be interdicted. The balloon was not sent up, due to its not being equipped with the necessary lights as required by the Department of Commerce. The airplane had been sent up to make the same adjustment just prior to the take-off of the Autogiro and, after having been up for over an hour, landed. Its crew reported they had not been able to locate the target or see the burst of a single shell, though they dropped one M-8 four-minute flare and four M-9 one-minute flares by parachute. The night was exceptionally dark, due to a haze and a complete overcast. In the Autogiro we succeeded in locating the target and obtained an excellent adjustment without dropping a single flare. Our observations were conducted from an altitude of about 4000 feet. They were very successful.

All concerned were not overencouraged with the results, however. For instance, this is the report one officer wrote and it is, to say the least, not very flattering to the Autogiro itself: "In these [night] problems both the airplane and the Autogiro were unrestricted as to zone of operation. The night chosen for these tests was very unfavorable for aerial adjustment because there was no moon, the visibility was poor, thundershowers were prevalent, lightning was flashing, and radio communication was poor on account of static. On this phase the airplane failed to secure an adjustment on two problems, but the Autogiro succeeded in its two missions. The reason for this is ascribed to the fact that the personnel in the Autogiro were much more experienced in night observation than were those in the airplane. No advantage whatever is conceded to the slow movement of the Autogiro."

There was truth in the statement.

Even the Battery Commander seemed to agree, for he remarked: "That guy up there in the Autogiro must have cat eyes. I'll be damned if I can see anything."

In a flight shortly after this I cracked up the YG-1—perhaps it would be more truthful to say it cracked me up—which brought an abrupt end to the tests at Fort Bragg. The accident was very much the same as Nick's. Just after a normal landing in which a slight roughness was noticed, I started to take off again when the rotor began vibrating terrifically and ultimately broke the pylon at its upper support just under the cowling, allowing the rotor hub to fall back over the cockpit and the blades to strike the ground and the fuselage. We shipped the aircraft back to the factory for another repair job. Meanwhile the Army took delivery of the new YG-1A and the craft was flown to Wright Field, near Dayton, Ohio, where we were going to run additional tests on it. Actually, the manufacturers blamed the two unfortunate accidents on "pilot error," and Nick and I were in for some "further training."

There were, indeed, many things we didn't know about the Autogiros.

The results of tests conducted at Fort Bragg were regarded merely as indications. In summary these were: The Autogiro, flying behind our own lines, was an efficient observation instrument for divisional artillery up to the limit of its range under good flying and visibility conditions. Under conditions of low visibility, such that the Autogiro can safely move beyond our front lines, as in night observations, it was a more efficient observation instrument than fast-flying conventional aircraft of that period. The airplane, due to its ability to fly to the target area during certain phases of combat, can locate and report targets with more facility than the Autogiro, which in turn possesses more facility in this respect than the balloon. For certain types of reconnaissance and for communication with ground troops, the Autogiro was superior to any current type of aircraft.

Yet, for all of this, it was definitely apparent that the Autogiro was not the ultimate answer. Regarding this, it is interesting to point to a report which I wrote in the closing month of 1936, setting forth some facts that clearly show I was thinking of another craft, a more efficient type that could do the things the Autogiro could do, but do them far better. The report reads:

"For the Autogiro to be of any value as an observation instrument, it will be absolutely essential for the craft to carry an observation load, such as radio, photographic equipment, pyrotechnics, charts and maps as necessary, with enough room to use these charts and maps. The present Autogiro can neither carry the weight of the required load, nor does it have room for any such load.

"I can see only one use of the present Autogiro: training of personnel in the art of handling and maintaining the Autogiro. Certainly it does not have any tactical value in its present form, as it will not carry a tactical load of equipment.

"With my limited experience with the Autogiro, I can visualize a very important value in the field of transportation. This Autogiro should be a two-place, side-by-side, enclosed-cockpit type. It should be capable of jumping to a height of fifty to one hundred feet; probably should have an endurance of two hours;

Front view of FW-61.

(which normally supports the blade when it is at rest) with such force that the blade deflected sufficiently to be cut by the whirling propeller.

Another time I was instructing a student how to come in over an obstacle and negotiate a quick landing. The last hangar on the line was selected as the obstacle, and we approached at a ninety-degree angle to the direction of wind. We scanned the landing area, turned into the wind, clearing the building's roof by a few feet in a steep glide. As we approached the ground I pulled back on the stick to flare the craft, the same maneuver as leveling off an airplane in a normal landing. Just then a man ran from underneath the fuselage. In this stage of the landing there was nothing to do but keep on coming down. A second later a tractor appeared directly ahead and to the left, and our Autogiro plumped down with one wheel on a golf-course-fairway gang mower, which the tractor was pulling. It was a narrow escape. The man and his machinery were not on the landing area prior to our turn, but drove onto it from out of the hangar after we had started our approach glide. By a strange incident, the man always stayed in the area blinded by the fuselage.

What was most unusual was the man's answer to my question: "Didn't you see the airplane approaching for a landing?"

"Sure, I saw it," he replied. "I've seen hundreds of 'em coming in just like that, but none of them danged others ever sat down this close to that building before."

He was amazed at the Autogiro's ability to land so sharply.

The rest of the Autogiro School was uneventful. Pilots and mechanics took their courses in stride and before long we had what could have been an Autogiro squadron—seven planes, twelve pilots, about fifteen mechanics. One day we had all the gyroplanes in the sky at the same time, flying in step formation. It was a beautiful sight, and newsreel men and press photographers were there to record the unusual formation. Then, I believe, the direct-control Autogiro got its first real taste of publicity. It was the beginning of a long build-up of interest by the general public in rotary-wing aircraft.

Shortly afterwards the graduates of the school went to Fort Monroe, Fort Sill, Fort Bragg, and conducted further tests with the ground services, the jobs they were trained for. I went to Wright Field to become project officer for all the Army's rotary-wing aircraft. The Matériel Division thought enough of the gyroplane and other similar craft to set up its own special branch, and some new plans for careful study of the problems were in progress. Generally it was conceded the Army would not buy any more of the then current types of gyroplanes. We would continue with tests of the ones already purchased, but merely with the idea of trying to improve them.

The greatest trend that occurred, however, was not with the Autogiro, nor with the results of the school, but with a nationwide interest in private flying. All over the country, airports were crowded with light-plane enthusiasts. It didn't take the Army experts long to realize that some of the small aircraft like the Aeronca, the Piper Cubs, Taylorcraft, Interstates, and Stinsons would do almost the same things in the air that the Autogiro could accomplish. The light planes were far cheaper. Tests were run with these craft in liaison problems with the ground forces during maneuvers. Results were very encouraging.

The words of my friend, the Field Artillery officer at Fort Sill, were being brought out more and more each day. The airplane was approaching the performance of the slow-flying Autogiro.

In truth, this had been done years before the advent of the Autogiro in the Army, since we had the famous Curtiss Tanager, winner of the Guggenheim Safe Airplane competition in 1929, which could fly as slow as thirty miles an hour, about the same as the Autogiro. Yet in the Autogiro we had seen a way to vertical flight and to many of us it seemed the next step toward the helicopter. Primarily this was the reason for the Army's gyro school and its exhaustive research into rotary-wing aircraft.

Thus one of my main tasks in the new job at Wright Field was to look for a successful helicopter.

9
The Army's Second Helicopter

W. LAURENCE LEPAGE was an engineer for the Pitcairn Autogiro Company and later for the Kellett Autogiro Company. Naturally he was completely sold on the future of rotary-wing aircraft. Havilland H. Platt, a mechanical engineer from New York, had been working for a long time with ideas for a cyclogyro and a helicopter. In 1938 the two got together and organized a company for the explicit purpose of building an aircraft capable of vertical flight. LePage went to Germany to pick up pertinent data on the successful Focke-Wulf craft. Both he and Platt had patents on similar ideas to those used in the German machine.

The background and knowledge of these two men gave birth to the Platt-LePage helicopter, the PL-3, the Army's first venture with the helicopter since de Bothezat. LePage, returned from Germany, came to Wright Field and showed movies of the FW-61 to the Army's already-interested engineers. Then, however, there were no funds available to go ahead with the craft which he proposed to build—a ship whose basic principle was the same as that of the German helicopter. Farsighted men of the Matériel Division, like their predecessor, Lieutenant Colonel Thurman H. Bane, who had brought about the first Army helicopter experiment nearly twenty years before, saw in LePage's suggested ideas the craft they were looking for. They wanted to try out the idea.

The money came unexpectedly. In those days when thoughts of national defense and war preparation were way down the line in the American mind, it was hard to get. On the floor of the House, Pennsylvania's Representative, Frank J. G. Dorsey, presented a bill (HR-8143) for the authorization and the appropriation of funds for the purpose of developing the Autogiro and procuring a sufficient number for service tests. When finally passed by the Seventy-fifth Congress on June 30, 1938, $2,000,000 was authorized to be appropriated to carry out studies and research in the development of rotary-wing and other aircraft. The actual wording of the bill was all-inclusive. Although it authorized appropriations for study of rotary-wing aircraft, the funds, if and when they were made available, could be used for the experimental development of a new bomber or a new fighter airplane (other aircraft). The Matériel Division was not to be

"gypped" of these funds for helicopter development if and when they were appropriated because of this "other aircraft."

The future was none too bright. Although $2,000,000 is a lot of money even in days when we are used to talking of billions, it is a mere atom of aluminum when measured in terms of aircraft research. Experimentation eats up dollars faster than the Flying Fortress eats up gasoline. For example, on the huge Douglas B-19 bomber, the world's largest landplane, the Army spent a sum in excess of $2,000,000 and the Douglas Company put in millions more. The Dorsey authorization was none too much.

Known officially as Act Public #787, the Dorsey Bill stated: "That in the interest of adequate national defense and the further interest of the needs of other governmental activities and of American commercial and civil aeronautics for rotary-wing and other aircraft development there is hereby authorized to be appropriated, out of any funds in the Treasury not otherwise appropriated, the sum of $2,000,000 to remain available until expended for the purpose of rotary-wing and other aircraft research, development, procurement, experimentation, and operation for service testing."

The Secretary of War was authorized and directed to proceed immediately with said program. Other agencies involved were: the Department of Agriculture's Bureau of Entomology and Plant Quarantine, Bureau of Biological Survey and the Forest Service, the Department of Interior's National Park Service, the Treasury Department's Coast Guard, the Department of Commerce's Bureau of Air Commerce, the Navy Department's Office of the Chief of Naval Operations, Bureau of Aeronautics and the Office of the Chief of the Marine Corps, the National Advisory Committee for Aeronautics, and the Post Office Department's Postmaster General. These agencies were urged to place special emphasis on the utility of rotary-wing and other aircraft at that time and to investigate "the promise this type of aircraft holds for the future in the opinion of the chief of each agency concerned."

When the money itself was obtained from the actual appropriation by Act Public #61 passed by the Seventy-sixth Congress almost a year later, the total sum was far less. Only $300,000 was made available. The Army was definitely decided—and since the

XR-1 at rest.

XR-1 in flight—Frank Gregory at controls.

Secretary of War was charged with the responsibility, this was unimpeachable—that it was going to spend the money on rotary-wing aircraft and, furthermore, the particular type of rotary-wing craft was to be the helicopter.

As they had done before on the public announcement of any Air Corps appropriation, inventors, enthusiasts, and manufacturers flocked to the Matériel Division at Wright Field, whose function, besides engineering, was also the approval and issuing of all Air Corps contracts through its Procurement Section. There were many closed-door conferences. Helicopter fanatics saw the golden egg even though it was small. One inventor claimed that the funds had been appropriated specifically for the development of his particular airplane and requested immediately that the sum of $1,750,000 be allotted to him so that he could finish his development.

This man and his brother had built a machine, all right. The amount of correspondence on the project would fill a book in itself, but it is an incident which I would like to mention here to show some of the trials of the Engineering Division. It has its humorous side too.

Lieutenant Victor R. Haugen, a graduate of the Autogiro School, now a full colonel, and I, under outside pressure alleging that we were neglecting some channels in the search for the proper rotary-wing aircraft, went to visit these inventors and to have a look-see at their creation. The men we met were amicable, good mixers, and talented, but definitely not engineers. One played the piano and the other was a violinist. They took us to their home and once inside they pulled down the shades and bolted the doors. We were, they informed us, about to hear of and see "the most secret and potentially the best helicopter ever designed by mankind." Then they brought out small rubber-band-powered models and flew them for us. One played the piano while the other flew the models which jumped up to the ceiling and bounced back down again as though they were dancing to the music.

It was highly amusing, but they were completely serious. Then we saw it. They had the craft stored in the back yard behind a high fence covered over with gunny sacks so that no one could peep through. There was a contraption. It was small, simulated a tiny airplane, had two wings as its rotor, and was apparently put together with stove bolts and cast-iron piping. They wheeled the craft out and, behind a police escort and heavy guard, took it to the near-by athletic field for a flight demonstration. Vic and I sat in the bleachers to watch it fly, if fly it could. It couldn't. The rotor, turned by a small motor, shook the craft and jounced it a little, but nothing happened which even remotely resembled flight.

We bade them farewell and went home.

On May 31, 1939, I attended a conference in the office of the Chief of the Air Corps with Colonel C. L. Tinker, who conducted the meeting in the absence of General Henry H. Arnold, then Chief of the Air Corps. This meeting had a great influence on the future of the helicopter. There were in attendance: J. P.

Godwin, Department of Agriculture; Frederick C. Lincoln, U. S. Biological Survey; Charles M. Kieobee, Division of Air Military Service; Captain L. T. Chalker, U. S. Coast Guard; John Easton, Civil Aeronautics Authority; Lieutenant Commander C. L. Helber, Bureau of Aeronautics; Roy Knabensheue, Department of the Interior; C. S. Helds and C. W. Crowley, Jr., of the NACA; Major W. C. Carter, Major D. G. Lingle, and Captain B. W. Chidlaw, from the Office of the Chief of the Air Corps; Captain Paul H. Kemmer, Matériel Division, Wright Field; Lieutenant Colonel W. D. Crittenberger, Cavalry; Major R. W. Beasley, Field Artillery; Lieutenant Colonel Dale D. Miniman, Coast Artillery; and Lieutenant Colonel E. W. Fales of the Infantry. These men laid the foundations for a new-type experimental rotary-wing aircraft.

J. P. Godwin of the Department of Agriculture, speaking for three different bureaus of that department, stated that a craft with a design useful load (that difference between weight empty and gross weight) of 1500 pounds, capable of carrying a crew of two with a two-and-a-half-hour gas capacity would meet with their general requirements. Other representatives said that any craft having air speeds from zero (hovering) up to 250 m.p.h. "desired" and a minimum top speed of 120 m.p.h., which could take off in or near vertical ascent and land from or near vertical descent, would meet their general requirements. It was decided that due to the limited funds available ($300,000) the Air Corps would develop a rotary-wing aircraft primarily as a machine incorporating all the novel features of this general type of aircraft, and that no attempt would be made in the first experimental article or articles to try to incorporate a military load, as required by the interested branches of the War Department, nor special facilities for the payloads required by other governmental agencies, until such a time as this type of craft had been proved.

Should a machine or machines of this type be developed (we were still dubious of the size), it could then be modified to meet the special requirements of the various interested agencies, provided it was capable of carrying a design useful load of 1200 to 1800 pounds. The helicopter was at the 1910 stage of the airplane, yet they wanted the Douglas Airliner model of the helicopter. It was felt by those engaged in the development that even a 1200-pound useful load was asking a little too much for the helicopter at that stage of its development.

In this special session we worked out the general specification and methods for evaluating designs. The aircraft industry was circularized and requested to submit designs and quotations for construction of a rotary-wing aircraft to meet the type specification. This was the routine procedure used by the government in securing new airplane designs. It was true of the Flying Fortress and it was true of every other bomber or fighter or glider or transport or trainer that the Air Corps asked for until the outbreak of war, when the "do it now or die" method was forced upon us by our enemies. Government Circular Proposal 40-260 asked for a rotary-wing aircraft. The method of evaluation definitely favored vertical flight.

XR-1A in flight.

Bids were opened on April 15, 1940, and there were only four designs received in compliance with the Circular Proposal—two offering to build Autogiros and two offering to build helicopters. Five other concerns submitted briefs, but these were not in accordance with the provisions and none contained design data, a prime requisite. In one case, only photographs of a model that *did not fly*, together with a statement that a helicopter *could be built from it*, were offered. Quotations from the bona fide bidders varied from slightly over $200,000 to more than $400,000 for one experimental airplane. The Platt-LePage Aircraft Company emerged winner of the competition. The design was thought the most practical, substantiated by the fact that an aircraft of its same basic principles had already flown successfully in Germany. The Army designated its new helicopter project, the XR-1 (experimental, rotary-wing aircraft model number one; the G designation was released since it did not cover representatively the rotary-wing aircraft field, and R substituted therefor—G is now used to designate gliders). Nineteen years after Professor George de Bothezat signed a contract to build his helicopter, which failed, the Air Corps, with renewed hope and faith, was venturing again into the realm of straight-up-and-down flight, buying its second helicopter.

The contract, No. 15375, with the Platt-LePage Aircraft Company of Eddystone, Pennsylvania, was approved by the Assistant Secretary of War on July 19, 1940, for the Army's second helicopter. The Air Corps pinned high hopes on the XR-1, particularly in view of the successful flights in Germany and the moderately successful flights of the superimposed coaxial twin-rotored helicopter designed and built by Louis Breguet in France. The helicopter, for all the skepticism, was approaching nearer and nearer to a definite practicable and usable machine. It had, after long years of defeat, actually flown with a good degree of

stability and control. Now it was a matter of developing it.

LePage promised the aircraft, according to contract, for delivery in January of the following year, 1941. The craft was already well under construction, for XR-1 had been started as the PL-3 in 1939 on a speculative basis, with the company putting up its own funds for experimentation. This aircraft was already familiar to those of us at Wright Field who were concerned with rotary-wing aircraft. Naturally it was part of our business to keep up-to-the-minute data on all such developments. LePage was enthusiastically co-operative on this. We made many visits to the factory. He came often to the field. This was long before we had any money for experimentation with the helicopter, and it was representative of civilian industry-Army cooperation—something which has saved our necks many times in these years of war; a tribute to American democracy.

The XR-1 is an aircraft weighing approximately 4800 pounds. It has a fuselage resembling very much a normal airplane fuselage, except that it has no engine and propeller at the nose. The tail is of conventional design and looks similar to the high-stabilizer big rudder empennage of a flying boat such as the Catalina. The engine is located approximately in the middle of the fuselage and is totally enclosed. Likewise, the two cockpits, located in the forward part of the craft in tandem, have sliding canopies over them, as have most of our fighters. The bottom of the pilot's and observer's compartment is transparent plastic to allow for clear vision when approaching from the vertical and to add to the helicopter's usefulness for observation purposes. Extending from each side of the fuselage, immediately to the rear of the two cockpits, is a streamlined pylon which gives the impression that it is a wing. At the end of each pylon is a rotor thirty and a half feet in diameter. The rotors are identical and rotate in oppo-

XR-1A in flight.

site directions, thus counteracting torque forces. The landing gear is conventional, having two main wheels and a tail wheel. All three wheels are free to caster. The craft is powered with a Pratt & Whitney R-985 engine developing 450 horsepower, the most powerful engine ever installed in a helicopter. This was the Platt LePage rotary-wing aircraft.

By the latter part of April, 1941, the aircraft was ninety-eight per cent completed. Only minor adjustments and the fitting of various pieces remained to be done. The manufacturer told me then he expected to run tests with the engine within a few days and probably would make a trial flight sometime within the next thirty days. Meanwhile, on the same trip East, I visited Igor Sikorsky, who was flying his own helicopter design, the VS-300, which was a small prototype of the XR-4 under construction for the Army Air Corps. Both the experiments were highly encouraging to those of us who knew the full weight of the problems involved in successful vertical flight. It was now almost certain that great strides had been made since Colonel Bane went through the similar trying years of experimentation with the de Bothezat.

On May 7, 1941, while at Cornell University in Ithaca, New York, addressing the graduating class of engineers and trying to get some of the nation's youngbloods to come to the Matériel Division with their ideas and talents, I received a wire from General George C. Kenney, then Chief of the Division and now MacArthur's supreme air commander in the South Pacific.

It read: RESTRAINED FLIGHT OF XR-1 BEING ATTEMPTED. CONTRACTOR WOULD APPRECIATE YOUR PRESENCE. I left immediately for Eddystone, arriving there two days before the XR-1 was ready for its initial take-off trials.

Lou Leavitt, who was the company's test pilot, formerly with Kellett, was ready for the occasion. The first flight of the XR-1 was to be made with the aircraft restrained by ropes. Thus the craft would be kept from lifting too high off the ground, since the manufacturer didn't want to take any risk of losing the aircraft or having it seriously damaged in this early stage of the tests.

The Platt LePage experimental shops were located just behind the big Baldwin Locomotive works in Eddystone, on the very banks of the Delaware River. It had been raining for two or three days, and when we went out to watch the tests, water filled the depressions in the surface of the tarmac strip behind the plant. Ropes were tied to the ends of the pylons and fastened to stakes in the ground. The XR-1 had been out here six times before, her rotors turned, and eager to take wing, but each time some minor trouble would develop and the flight would have to be postponed. This day, May 12, 1941, everything was in readiness. The craft was checked and checked again. Finally Lou Leavitt in the cockpit gave her half throttle and the ship lifted into the air, tugging at the ropes which held her. The Army's second helicopter was air-borne.

Present for the demonstration was a famous aeronautical figure, Grover Loening, who was at that time a consultant for the Platt-LePage Company. When he saw the ship actually in the air he turned to me and remarked: "This craft has tremendous possibilities, but there is still a long hard way ahead."

This was true. The XR-1 had flown, but it still had not proved itself beyond that degree of success which other helicopters had obtained previously. That we knew of the trials which lay ahead is brought out in the fact that Matériel Division experts were seriously considering turning the static test model of the XR-1, which was called for in the contract, into a flyable craft as a precaution against destruction of the XR-1 then making restrained flights. The men at Wright Field were well aware that in several instances much work and time had been lost when only one experimental article was procured. On October 30, 1935, they had seen the only model of the first Flying Fortress, the Boeing 229, Army XB-17, crash, after only fifteen hours of flying at Wright Field, during tests nearly eliminating the craft from our list of standard bombers. Many thought the XB-17 too big for a human pilot to fly. Only through farsighted recommendations based on previous experience did we go ahead with a service test order on the B-17's, which Matériel Division engineers saw "as one of the greatest planes ever built," despite its unfortunate start. Without their "know-why," that umbrella of Forts might not be over Germany these days. Yes, they knew, and they wanted to make sure in the case of the helicopter. After hot debates, however, they decided that the static test model would be more valuable for the purpose procured.

Almost every aircraft we buy has a static test model built practically simultaneously with the first flight test model. It is usually shipped to Wright Field, where the men in the Aircraft Laboratory subject it to strenuous structural tests. Sand-filled or shot-filled bags are piled on its wings and fuselage to see how much it can take. Hydraulic-pressure jacks and suction cups pull at its skin and framework, trying to twist and break it. Literally they try to tear the aircraft apart—to see what would happen to it in a violent gale, how much weight it can stand, how violent a maneuver it can take. If it withstands the tests, the aircraft is pronounced structurally sound. It has undergone on the ground in the test routine far more than it would ever be called upon to stand in actual flight. That is just one of the safety factors that go into every military airplane. In the case of the XR-1 the craft took its punishment and came out with the Army's okay.

Less than a week after its first flight, the XR-1 made a free flight. That day I received a call from LePage, who was quite excited.

"Frank," he said, "we flew it last night and it was quite successful, though there are quite a few bugs in the thing that will have to come out before we can do any real flying."

"How long was it off the ground?" I asked.

"Never more than thirty seconds."

"How high did it go?"

"About three feet, I guess, at a maximum."

Platt-LePage was still in the class with Pescara, d'Ascanio, and others who had attempted to fly helicopters. It would fly for a short time, make several flights a few feet off the ground, then

VS-300 in her first successful configuration—Igor Sikorsky up.

VS-300 in her second successful configuration—Les Morris up.

The XR-3 (modified YG-1).

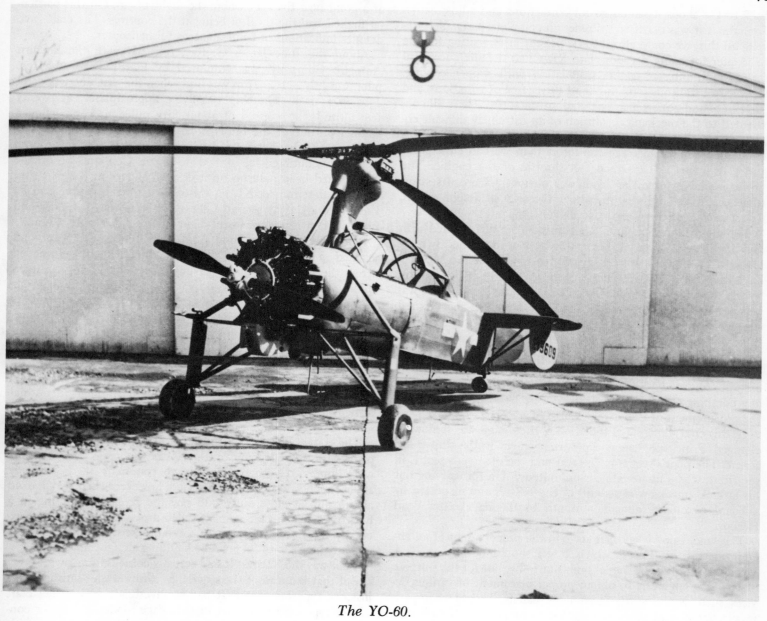

The YO-60.

The XR-4 tries it again with covering on.

Frank Gregory's first flight in the VS-300.

XR-4 as she was rolled out for the first time beside VS-300.

XR-4 (left) and VS-300 (final configuration) in formation.

of the craft.

The landing gear—vertical hydraulic shock struts which were strut-braced and extended to the left and right sides of the craft at ninety-degree angles to the engine mount—supported the aircraft on two small balloon-tired wheels. A tiny wheel in the tail supported the craft from that position.

This was the XR-4.

It took Sikorsky mechanics and test engineers about a month to make ground tests and preliminary runs with the new helicopter. They tested the engine thoroughly and got the blades properly balanced and controlled. A few structural changes and weight changes were effected here and there, but generally the craft kept its same shape and weight as it had the day they first brought it out in the open. They did, however, feel that it would not be wise to fly it without putting some additional cushioning on the nose and as a result of this a makeshift fourth wheel ar-

rangement was devised. A pair of small dolly wheels were rigged up on a two-by-four plank which was bolted to the bottom of the craft to protect it in case of a nose-over.

Sikorsky's chief test pilot, Les Morris, who had flown most of the tests with the VS-300 during the elimination of the horizontal rotors and who had been with the company since the XR-4 was started, was nominated to fly the Army's vertical-flight craft. Morris flew the ship on the morning of January 14, 1942. He made a total of six test flights that day, the longest of which lasted for seven minutes and twenty seconds. Total flying time was twenty-five minutes and six seconds for all the flights—a short period, but a milestone in the development of the helicopter in this country. While there were many changes to be made, the flights indicated definitely that the craft would be successful. The Army could claim a new first with its initial flight of the XR-4.

12
The Demonstration

"YOU, GENTLEMEN," Les Morris explained, "are about to witness a demonstration of the first successful basically single-rotor helicopter in the world."

It was a mixed group to whom he talked. In addition to Major Leslie B. Cooper, Mandel Lenkowsky and the author, representing the Matériel Division, there were: Allen W. Morris of the Civil Aeronautics Authority; F. J. Bailey of the National Advisory Committee for Aeronautics; Commander W. J. Kossler of the U. S. Coast Guard; L. M. Nesbitt; Wing Commander R. A. C. Brie of the British Air Commission; Commander J. H. Millar of the Royal Navy; Colonel George L. King and Lieutenant Colonel P. E. Gabel of the Armored Force Section of the Ground Forces. All were present to see a flight demonstration of the XR-4 aircraft to be given in accordance with the requirements of Article 18 in the contract with the Vought-Sikorsky Company.

By the contract it was specified that "the aircraft called for will be demonstrated by the contractor at a flying field to be approved by the government in the vicinity of the contractor's plant. Such demonstration shall be conducted by the contractor at his expense and risk and shall prove to the government the airworthiness and structural integrity of said aircraft."

The site approved by the government for the tests was a small meadow about one hundred yards from the Sikorsky plant, in Stratford, Connecticut. The date was April 20, 1942. Les Morris was to be pilot on the series of flights. It was a gray, crispy cold day, but practically all of the Sikorsky workers who had built the craft and, of course, Igor Sikorsky himself turned out to see the trials.

The field was especially prepared for the tests. A square approximately twenty feet each side was marked off on the edge of the grass; all landings and take-offs were accomplished in this area without any run whatsoever on the ground. There was a gusty wind of approximately ten miles per hour blowing across the meadow, making the task of controlling the aircraft more difficult than if there had been a steady breeze or a calm.

The demonstration began with several vertical ascents and descents. The first time Les jumped the craft straight up to about seven feet and held it there motionless over our heads. After several minutes he let the craft settle back down gradually right on the same spot so close that the wheels fitted perfectly in the shallow grooves they had dug in the soft spring sod. Next he

took off and went about twice as high as the first time. Then he flew the ship sideways, much to the amazement of the onlookers who were unfamiliar with this type of craft. He made it go backwards. He flew forwards. He went up and down like an elevator, barely touching the ground on the descents. Then he brought the XR-4 down ever so gently and stepped from the cockpit to accept congratulations from all who saw it.

Various comments were made by the different members of the group.

The British Wing Commander said to me: "That chap"—he laughed—"has flown your rotor machine and what he's done, I say, beats anything I've ever observed. We've really seen something this day. I shall send a signal to my country stating the full import of this great event."

Another one of the witnesses remarked: "If I hadn't seen it with my own eyes I'd say what just took place was impossible."

My associate Major Leslie B. Cooper cracked: "Greg, you're right. That thing will do anything a horse can do."

Igor Sikorsky was all smiles.

One thing was certain. As far as its general flight characteristics were concerned—that is, how well it could take off and land, how sensitive it was to the controls—the XR-4 left no doubt in anyone's mind that it was up to this date the most successful helicopter ever flown in this country. For that matter it was the most practical helicopter in the world.

There followed a series of tests to illustrate the accurateness of the control of the craft. A couple of mechanics placed a pole, which was about eight feet high, in the ground a short distance from the marked area. They attached to it a ring about ten inches in diameter much in the same fashion as the brass ring sticks out on the arm on the merry-go-round at a carnival. Les was going to try for a "free ride." Back in the air again, he hovered the craft at an altitude just slightly over the height of the pole. Then delicately he controlled and inched forward, attempting to slip the Pitot-static tube (used in measuring the air speed) through the ring and fly away again. He made it the first time, scoring a bull's-eye. Then he brought the helicopter over to its inventor, Igor Sikorsky, and dropped the craft to within an arm's length from Igor's head. The inventor reached up and took the ring off the tube, handing it to Bob Labensky.

The incident reminded me of a boy and his dog. He had thrown away a stick. The animal had retrieved it and brought it back to its master. This strange craft was, indeed, almost a living thing.

Next, a net bag containing a dozen eggs was suspended from the Pitot-static tube at the end of a ten-foot rope. Responding delicately to its controls the XR-4 took off gradually. The slack in the rope was taken up and the craft lifted the bag of eggs out of the hands of a pretty secretary who had come to take notes on the demonstration. Morris, who was flying the aircraft, circled for a minute, then descended so smoothly that the bag of eggs was placed on the ground without an egg being broken.

Someone kidded: "They're probably hard-boiled eggs and wouldn't break, anyway."

Bob Labensky heard the remark and didn't like it. Without saying a word he walked over to the basket, picked out one egg, cracked it on a rock. The egg was raw.

The XR-4 had proved she was as gentle as a mare.

Some indication of the potential utility of this type of aircraft was brought out in the next phase of the demonstration. Les Morris and Bob Labensky, flying in the XR-4, lowered a telephone to Sikorsky and me on the ground and we carried on a conversation with Bob, probably the first ground-to-air telephone communication ever accomplished in a helicopter. Since the aircraft was only about twenty-five feet high at all times during the conversation, the exhaust from its engine made it difficult to hear, but generally our voices carried well over the wire and it was comparatively easy to understand one another. While he was talking to me, Bob Labensky was also making sketches of various objects and sliding them down the telephone wire on small loop hooks. It demonstrated the practicability of helicopter communication with ground commanders if the craft were ever used as we had already tried to use the Autogiro in its long series of tests.

Following the telephone communication, a rope ladder was attached to the cabin of the XR-4 and, assuming no clearing sufficient for a landing, tests were made to show how easy it was to pick up a passenger by merely hovering overhead. The craft took off and circled the field; returning to its original take-off spot. At that moment the pilot lowered the rope ladder and Ralph Alex, a Sikorsky engineer, climbed up the rungs into the ship's cockpit. The craft flew around the field again and returned to let its passenger descend the same way as he had climbed into the craft. The whole stunt was done without any more danger than a man encounters when he is painting a high wall from the top of a ladder. On another similar trial the rope ladder was dispensed with and the aircraft came down to within twenty or twenty-five feet of the ground, hovered there almost motionless while its passenger opened the door, lowered a rope, and lowered himself to the ground. Both these tests illustrated how the XR-4 might be used for evacuation of personnel in isolated spots such as jungles and how it could deliver key personnel to ground installations like an aerial taxi.

The demonstration was concluded with several flights of the VS-300 mounted on inflated bags instead of conventional landing gear. It made several take-offs from the field and landed on the Housatonic River, then took off again and flew back to the demonstration area. It was evident that the floats were practicable for almost any kind of landing on any kind of terrain, and it was decided at the demonstration that the XR-4 would be equipped with similar pneumatic floats for further tests.

When the exhibition trials were over, the following wire was sent to General Carroll, Chief of the Engineering Division at Wright Field:

FLIGHT DEMONSTRATION OF XR-4 MOST SUCCESSFUL. THE CRAFT DEMONSTRATES ALL THAT COULD BE ASKED OF THE HELICOPTER TO SATISFACTION OF ALL WITNESSES. ALTITUDE REACHED DURING DEMONSTRATION, FIVE THOUSAND FEET, EXPECT XR-4 DELIVERY TO WRIGHT ON OR ABOUT MAY FIRST. GREGORY.

The Army had a successful helicopter.

It was true that the demonstration had impressed those who saw it far beyond their wildest expectations. When it was completed, many discussions ensued among the representatives of the various government agencies and the Vought-Sikorsky people about the future of the helicopter. All agreed that further development of the Vought-Sikorsky helicopter should be carried on as soon as possible.

The Army unhesitatingly pointed out to all concerned that there were many uses for an aircraft of this type. Some of these were:

CONVOY DUTY: Helicopters should be suited for convoying merchant ships, for they can take off and land vertically without forward speed and can be operated directly from decks of ships they are convoying. Several methods are available for such operations. It should be practicable to remove the landing gear from the helicopter and erect a cradle on the deck of the merchant ship into which the helicopter could settle. In the event of rough seas, the helicopter could drop a line to the deck of the ship and be drawn down into the cradle by a winch. A number of helicopters attached to a convoy could maintain a highly effective antisubmarine patrol.

COASTAL AND HARBOR PATROL: Due to the helicopter's ability to fly slowly or hover at will, an effective antisubmarine and mine patrol could be maintained over coastal and harbor regions.

OBSERVATION AND FIRE CONTROL: The unique characteristics of the helicopter make it superior to all other methods of observation and fire control. As demonstrated, it is feasible to carry on conversation between the helicopter and the ground and to lower maps and sketches to the ground. This feature of the craft would also be ideal for Forest Ranger work in the wooded areas of the nation. The helicopter on regular patrol duty might replace the giant firetowers that spot the hillsides in these sections of the country. It too would be ideal for lowering fire fighters into the danger areas, possibly quenching a conflagration before it had a chance to get out of hand.

LIAISON AND COMMUNICATIONS: The helicopter could operate from any open terrain having approximately a twenty foot square of relatively smooth space and does not require more open space for operation than approximately three or four times its own dimensions. Thus the helicopter could operate from practically any open space and perform valuable service for courier work with rapidly moving mechanized forces.

AMBULANCE DUTIES: The helicopter can operate between advanced positions and base hospitals without depending on prepared landing fields. It can be of vital service transporting wounded personnel and medical supplies.

Besides these major applications the helicopter could be used in other ways: wire laying for communications, photography, rescue missions, laying of smoke screens, transport of personnel and light cargo between otherwise inaccessible positions, and traffic control.

Although there was only one experimental military helicopter in existence, the XR-4, and that still undelivered to the Army, the records of the performance that had already been demonstrated gave every indication that such craft as this would definitely sometime in the near future be capable of performing a multitude of tasks. From the demonstration and other tests we learned that the XR-4 could obtain forward speed of seventy-eight miles per hour without using the full power output of the engine. It had reached an altitude of 5000 feet and part of the descent was made with power off, the aircraft functioning as a gyroplane.

It was not difficult to draw far-reaching conclusions:

The XR-4 was a successful and practical helicopter, capable of true vertical flight, hovering, forward, backward, and sideways flight;

Aircraft of this type had a definite military value which should be exploited to the greatest possible extent and as quickly as possible;

Construction of helicopters larger than the XR-4 was practicable and was the next logical step in the program of helicopter development;

The XR-4 aircraft was capable of carrying a depth charge (an underwater bomb) for shipboard operation by removing the observer.

With these somewhat obvious and demonstrated features clearly in mind and freshly back from having seen the XR-4 perform miracles, I wrote a report to the Chief of the Engineering Division at Wright Field, setting forth the following recommendations:

That service-test helicopters similar to the XR-4 be procured without delay to familiarize Army Air Force personnel with helicopter operation and maintenance and to determine all the uses of these craft;

That helicopter development be continued on a much larger scale;

That experimental contracts be entered into with Vought-Sikorsky Aircraft Division for helicopters having a larger useful load than the XR-4, the larger helicopters to be capable of carrying depth charges, aerial mines, or other armament.

It was these recommendations which later gave birth to the YR-4, the XR-5, and the XR-6 Sikorsky helicopters. But there were other significant trends in those recommendations. They pointed certainly toward an expansion program for helicopter development. The days of the skeptics were gone. The helicopter was here to stay.

13
The XR-4 Goes West

THERE WAS CONSIDERABLE debate on the subject. By the terms of the contract the Vought-Sikorsky people were to deliver the XR-4 to the Army at Wright Field. Would it be flown in? Or would it be crated and shipped by highway truck? Igor Sikorsky felt that this "first-of-the-type" should be shipped, thus eliminating the potential hazards of cross-country flight in a totally novel type of aircraft which had less than twenty flying hours to its credit at the time it was slated for delivery.

The decision to fly the helicopter cross-country rested with the Army. It was decided that the craft should be flown to Wright Field. This was based first upon the idea that it would afford an excellent opportunity to obtain heretofore unknown data on a craft of this type and, secondly, because those of us who had followed its development were convinced it could accomplish the feat. A week prior to the flight I was at the Sikorsky plant, working out the details to bring the XR-4 to Dayton. There were two routes to be considered. One was 560 miles and the other was 760 miles. To make the shorter trip would put the helicopter over rough mountain ranges. Because open fields were more inviting than mountainsides, it was decided to fly the extra 200 miles through the Mohawk Valley, which meant practically flat country over the entire route.

Eleven stops in all were scheduled—New Hackensack, Albany, Utica, Syracuse, Rochester, Buffalo, Erie, Cleveland, Mansfield, Springfield, and Wright Field. Actually, before the flight was completed there were several additional stopovers. It was estimated that the trip would be most efficiently made at an average altitude of 1000 feet at approximately sixty miles per hour. That was how it was all worked out—the first cross-country flight in a helicopter in the Western Hemisphere; the first delivery flight of such a craft in the world. Les Morris was to fly the XR-4 west to Wright Field.

The flight began on May 13, 1942, in a little triangular meadow close to the Vought-Sikorsky Aircraft plant in Stratford, Connecticut, the same field from which the XR-4 had made her initial flight not so long before. It was a bright morning, with a warm gentle spring breeze which barely rustled the newborn leaves on the long rows of stately elms which bordered the field. Practically all of the plant's employees who had been engaged in work on the Army's helicopter were grouped along the road which cut

through the triangle. Their eyes were focused on test pilot Morris as he readied the ship for take-off. Except for these witnesses, who were comparatively few, this was to be no public demonstration. The military had no respect for the writers of history, for this was a historic event shrouded in secrecy.

Many of Morris' friends came out to the craft and wished him the best of luck. His boss, Igor Sikorsky, came out to the ship and thrust out his hand: "Well, Les," he said, "today you are making history." Serge Gluhareff, who is assistant engineering manager for the plant, added his best wishes: "Les, I have asked God to bless you."

Morris gave her the throttle and the ship lifted vertically to about twelve feet; then as he eased forward on the control stick the craft started off across the field, her nose slightly pointed downward, going at a healthy clip. He came back and circled low over the heads of those who had come to witness the start of the flight, then he slowly climbed the helicopter to 1500 feet and pointed its nose to the west, the sun to follow the trail of his tail rotor.

Only a short time before the helicopter roared away, a car, with a big yellow bull's-eye painted on its top, sped through the factory gate. For five days it was to shadow the helicopter. It was like the cruisers and destroyers that marked the way across the Atlantic for the NC-4 flying boat in 1919. In purpose, at least, it was the same. In it were Bob Labensky, project engineer, who had cast his lot with the penniless Sikorsky nineteen years before; Ralph Alex, his assistant, who had labored endless days and nights to bring this craft to flying condition; Adolph Plenefisch, shop foreman, and Ed Beaty, the company's transportation chief, who elected to drive the party. Their job was to be on hand with the tools and know-how in case anything should go wrong with the craft, necessitating a forced landing en route. Thus any delays would be minimized.

The first landmark, coincidentally enough, was Igor Sikorsky's home. Morris wanted to land the craft in the front lawn, so that, for a matter of record, the first successful helicopter on the first cross-country flight in our half of the world would make its first stop en route by landing in the yard of the ship's own creator. It would have been a fine gesture, but Morris flew on, passing over Newton, where his own parents lived, and thence to Danbury, where a checkup showed the ship was a little behind the rotor blade is rotating, a force resulting from rotation is developed, known as centrifugal force, which is the same force that is felt in your hand when a rock is whirled on the end of a string. This force tends to hold the blade straight out. The lift force tends to lift the blade. At a certain position of the blade which is only a few degrees above the horizontal, these two forces balance out or are in equilibrium. This position of the blade or the angle the blade makes with the horizontal is known as the coning angle. When the blade flaps, this coning angle varies during the cycle of rotation of the blade.

The pitch of the helicopter's blades can also be controlled collectively, which means changing the pitch of all three blades at the same time. This is done only to absorb properly the power of the engine. It can be done automatically. But at present in the Sikorsky helicopters there is a lever known as the collective-pitch-control handle. This lever is operated with an up and down motion and when it is pulled up it increases the pitch of all blades equally. When pushed down, it decreases the pitch of all blades equally. The automatic mechanism for accomplishing this will operate when the throttle is opened or closed in the same manner in which constant-speed propellers are controlled on an airplane.

The rudder pedals on the Sikorsky helicopters vary the pitch of the blades of the small rotor on the tail of the aircraft. This rotor, which rotates in a vertical plane, is primarily for torque counteraction; however, it is also used to control the craft about its vertical axis or directionally. This control is actuated by increasing or decreasing the thrust delivered by this rotor (the thrust is varied by changing the pitch), which force pulls the tail in one direction or allows torque to turn it in the opposite direction. Torque is that force which tends to turn the body of the aircraft in the opposite direction to which the main rotor is turning.

Yet for all its control devices, its whirling blades, its vertical rotor, its pitch-changing mechanisms, what makes the helicopter go sideways, back up, go forward, climb, descend? As we look at the aircraft in the air there is no visible means of support, though we know that it is being held up there on a column of air the blades are thrusting downward.

Assume that the helicopter is being supported by a single cable running through the center of the rotor disk or through the hub of the rotor. This string or cable is the resultant vector of lift or thrust. This lift vector always tends to remain perpendicular to the rotor disk. If we move the stick forward and change the pitch of the blades cyclically in such a manner as to cause the rotor disk to tilt forward, then the lift vector will also tilt forward, and therefore the helicopter moves in that direction. The center of gravity of the aircraft is always under this lift vector and tends to keep in line with it, which is the reason that the fuselage of the helicopter practically always maintains its same relative position to the rotor disk. In other words, as the rotor disk tilts sideways, so does the fuselage; as the rotor disk tilts backward, so does the fuselage. This action takes place because

of the axiom that the center of gravity always seeks the line of lift. Consequently, as the lift vector is tilted in any direction, the center of gravity of the aircraft moves so as to be on the rotor thrust line.

The center of gravity of any object or body is that point under which the body may be balanced. It is the point of equilibrium. If the body is suspended, the center of gravity will always be under the point of suspension.

Another method of control for the helicopter is to tilt the hub rather than change the pitch of the blades cyclically. The YG-1 Autogiro was controlled in this manner. The rotating hub was actually tilted. The helicopter can be controlled in a like manner.

Still another means of control employs separate control rotors, which was the way Igor Sikorsky first successfully flew the VS-300 helicopter. In this instance, there is no control in the main rotor at all, except collective pitch control for proper power absorption. The aircraft is controlled longitudinally by increasing or decreasing the upward thrust of two horizontal rotors located on the tail of the plane. To control the craft laterally, the thrust of one of these rotors is increased, while the thrust of the other is decreased. Again, this action has the same effect as the movement of the ailerons.

A helicopter may have twin rotors. These rotors should turn in opposite directions to counteract torque forces. The rotors may be superimposed—that is, one over the other—or laterally disposed in the same plane, longitudinally disposed in the same plane or in different planes. Or a twin rotor craft may have its rotors extending laterally and the blades intermeshing, similar to an egg beater. Directional control of a twin-rotor helicopter, if the rotors are superimposed, can be obtained by increasing the pitch of the blades of one rotor and decreasing the pitch of the other, thus causing greater torque in one rotor and the ship to turn in that direction. By reversing the action the craft will

XR-4 landing on platform, twenty by twenty feet.

XR-4 stops for a moment for one of her crew to leave camera.

turn in the opposite direction. In the laterally or longitudinally disposed twin-rotor helicopter, directional control is obtained by tilting the lift vector of one rotor in one direction and the lift vector of the other rotor in the opposite direction, which will cause the craft to turn.

There are other methods of controlling helicopters, but basically all are a variation of the types mentioned above. The helicopter flies, as the airplane flies, due to the forces acting upon it being created by the motion of its blades through the air. It is far from being a simple device. Quite the contrary, it is a complex, intricate mechanism. This, more than anything else, accounts for the long, trying years of research and engineering which have been necessary to bring it into the realm of the practical.

15
Tests at Wright Field

THE SPECTACULAR DOESN'T determine an airplane's worth. Seldom does it win wars. It is a poor slide rule with which to measure the performance of anything, especially an airplane. An engineer will not accept it. He is wont to probe; to take a thing apart and find out how it ticks. That was the way the Matériel Center (later changed to Matériel Command), which is alive with the best aeronautical engineers you can find anywhere, civilian or military, felt about the XR-4. The helicopter was spectacular. By its very design and the success of that design it was indeed unique. That it flew at all made it more so. The cross-country flight it had just made put it in a category with aviation's firsts. Wright Field had many firsts. Its men had made them. They had taken them apart, put them under a series of microscopes, put them back together again, and flown them for the better. What they didn't learn on the ground they wrung out of the planes in the air. They were going to do the same with the helicopter.

How high would the helicopter go? How does altitude affect the craft's control? How fast would it go? Was there sufficient control for all conditions of flight one might encounter? Could it take it in maneuvers? Of what maneuvers was it capable? What were its weak points? The engineers of the Matériel Center at Wright Field were going to find out the answers to these questions. What they learned would decide the future of the XR-4 and all other helicopters.

The job was mine: to supervise, direct, and perform the rigid tests scheduled and do it quickly so that the Army would know where it stood in the field of helicopter development. The program as planned was to include: flights to altitude, endurance flights, speed calibrations, power calibration, maneuverability trials, controllability tests, and utility trials.

It was a job that would require precise and exact flying. More, too, it meant that the XR-4 had to go to the shops where Army mechanics installed a galaxy of test instruments, including baragraphs to record accurately atmospheric pressure during the various tests.

My specific task was not only to direct the program, but to fly the ship on the tests as well. The many years that I had spent fathering the helicopter and the Autogiro into existence dictated that by right of experience. It was more than just being a test pilot, for normal test flights are done by the expert pilots of the Engineering Division's Flight Section, who had tested every type of airplane the Army has and some that it doesn't own yet. With this type of craft I could probably get the most out of the ship in the tests. Les Morris had run many of the initial flight investigation tests at Stratford, but his trials did not bring out the maximum performance that was in the ship. He was merely interested to find out that the aircraft could meet the already mentioned nonrigid requirements of the contract. The XR-4 had done that. On May 30, 1942, she was officially accepted by the Army, which wasn't satisfied with merely her good report card, but wanted to know more about her conduct after classes.

The bombing capabilities of the XR-4 were among the first tests. There had been much speculation on the use of the helicopter as an antisubmarine weapon. The long list of Atlantic sinkings scored in the spring of that year turned the attention of military strategists toward this novel idea for combating the underseas raiders. Many had thought the gyroplane would do the job. Some even advocated that light planes equipped with floats and catapulted from a tanker might ward off subs. Naturally, Army men who had nursed the helicopter to success saw it as the ideal craft for such operations. There remained one big question: besides spotting a submarine, could it drop depth charges on the raider?

Working with Colonel Douglas M. Kilpatrick (killed in a crash on September 8, 1942), then director of the Bombardment Branch of the Engineering Division's Armament Laboratory, we readied the helicopter for her trials as a bomber. Doug was quick to see the possibilities of this hovering craft for bombing and enthusiastically co-operated in getting the necessary bomb sights and bomb racks fabricated and installed. While actual work on these facilities was in progress, several flights were made with the ship to get some preliminary indications as to the ability of the XR-4 to hover and drop bombs.

The very first tests were made by taking off with a passenger who held a twenty-five-pound dummy bomb in his lap. An outline of a submarine was drawn with chalk powder on one side of the field and the helicopter would hover over the "sub"; then at a given signal from the pilot, the passenger holding the bomb over the side of the ship would let it go. This was very crude, indeed, but it gave us an idea of what to expect. Since these tests were made at from fifty to four hundred feet and without any sighting equipment, not the best possible accuracy was obtained. Some of the bombs came within three feet of the target. Others missed by thirty yards. While doing this practice bombing, the XR-4 did not land. It would come down to within a few feet of the ground, hover there motionless for a moment, as another bomb was handed up; then off it would go for another practice drop.

When the aircraft was equipped for bombing, the results were more accurate. A bomb sight much the same as the pendulum-type bomb sight used on some of our early bombers was installed on the outside of the cabin, so the pilot in order to use it had to crane his neck out a window just as you would use a mirror on a truck. Underneath the fuselage were bomb racks fitted to carry five of the twenty-five-pounders. The bombs were released by a trigger on the stick which clicked off an automatic release device. Using this method, the bombing was more accurate and hits were scored in the center of an old piece of oil-cloth that was used to represent the conning tower of the submarine. However, it was soon learned that the most accurate bombing was not accomplished from a hovering position over the target. This was due chiefly to the fact that it was practically impossible to tell the exact location of the ship over the target. A bombing run on the target at a slow speed, approximately forty miles per hour, proved more accurate.

A report was made on the bombings to General Carroll, who returned it to me with the remark scribbled at the bottom: "Haven't you fellows sunk that sub yet?"

In this report to General Carroll it was explained: "These tests are being run merely as indications of the helicopter's ability to drop depth charges on a submarine that is below the surface. It is fully realized that subs with antiaircraft protection, as they are now reported having, would be able to knock the helicopter out of the air almost before it could get within range to drop its charges. However, test results indicate that the craft is capable of carrying a depth charge and that this can be dropped with a fair degree of accuracy."

The farsightedness and the keen observing mind of General Henry H. Arnold, Chief of the Air Forces, dictated his extreme interest in the XR-4 helicopter. The man who today has done and is doing an unparalleled job of organization and handling of the greatest potential military force ever assembled in history was so interested in the future of vertical flight that he took time out while on a special trip to Wright Field on July 7, 1942, to witness demonstration flights that we put on for him in the Army's first successful helicopter.

The XR-4 came near not being ready for the General. A few days before, mechanics during an over-all inspection found that the transmission gears were badly burned because of a clogged oiling system. Naturally the ship was grounded. This was four days before the General was scheduled to arrive to see the demonstration. There were no spare gears available at Wright Field, so it meant a rush job to get the craft back in the air again. When we learned of the General's visit, the gears were at the Sikorsky plant being repaired. The problem was to get them back to Dayton in time and installed in the ship.

Ralph P. Alex and Adolph Plenefisch at the Sikorsky plant, when they received my telephone call asking that the gearbox be rushed to completion, had their problems. It was the Fourth of July and nobody was working at the plant. Consequently they had to scrape up workers, do the engineering details themselves, and finally after all day and all night they got the gears ready for shipment. Then they personally made the delivery. With a heavy gearbox and other paraphernalia necessary for its installation, they boarded a TWA airliner for the flight to Dayton, Ohio. That day a gearbox for a helicopter ousted two angry passengers from their plush seats so it could make the flight instead. The thing wouldn't fit in the baggage compartment. A few hours later it was at Wright Field and on the morning of the seventh, after another sleepless night on the part of Alex and Plenefisch, the XR-4 was ready to strut her stuff for General Arnold.

This incident is mentioned here because it is so indicative of the fine spirit of co-operation between the Army and the manufacturer that existed all during the development of the helicopter. Without it the machine might still be in its shell of infancy.

I put the XR-4 through the usual maneuvers for General Arnold's party: a few short flights—backward, forward, sideways. He was greatly impressed, but at that time very noncommittal. Yet later in Washington, when we were discussing production of the new and larger helicopters, the R-5's, even before the first experimental model of this type had flown, he said: "The Army Air Forces has taken fliers before with not so much to gain promised. I think we're justified in doing it again in this case." What he meant was "Go ahead; procure the craft right from the drawings, if necessary." Undoubtedly his faith was established that July 7 when he saw the XR-4 perform.

The tests continued.

Take-offs and landings were next. This is part of every airplane's routine testing at the Matériel Division. It is more like a Hollywood setting for the filming of *The Great Train Robbery* than anything else because it involves motion-picture crews atop mobile trucks and in film shacks spread out over the flying field as though they were about to film the scene when Tom Mix and Tony go racing after the villain. Actually there is a specified course mapped out over which the airplane must fly. At a certain spot the pilot begins to land his plane. The camera begins to grind, catching every motion of the aircraft and the exact instant that its wheels touch the ground, and follows its roll until the machine comes to a stop. The same thing is done on the take-off: a cameraman follows the ship with his lenses until there is light under its wheels, tails it to altitude so that the whole take-off is recorded on movie film. When the film is edited and carefully pieced together, experts can tell exactly the minimum distance needed for take-off and also for landings. It is an invaluable characteristic that can be written into the handbook of operating instructions on every type airplane. Matériel Command engi-

Frank Gregory speaks to the Secretary of War, The Honorable Mr. Henry Lewis Stimson after flight demonstration of XR-4.

neers ingeniously devised this movie-film technique, which has saved many hundreds of hours and makes for greater accuracy.

Running these tests on the XR-4 was rather humorous since the craft takes off vertically and descends the same way. But engineers persisted: how straight up? And they proceeded to find out by using the cameras.

One cameraman, who had been filming the fastest ships only an hour before, when he saw the helicopter perform, turned away in disgust: "I may as well throw this fast-lens job away and go back to my Brownie."

The film was positive proof: the helicopter could take off and land *vertically*.

It was during these motion-picture runs that XR-4 nearly met disaster. I think to this day that the Omnipotent had a controlling hand in the matter, as had been the case several times before. The ship was positioned in the center of the runway being used for the take-off and landing tests. The rotors were turning at an idling speed, and I was waiting for the signal from the cameraman. Suddenly the helicopter without any warning took a lunge to the right as if blown by a strong gust of wind. In this case "the wind" was the high speed rush of a P-47 Thunderbolt going better than 100 miles per hour, whose pilot, without making radio contact, came in for his landing on the test runway. He had not seen the XR-4 and the silver wing of the fighter passed under the big rotor of the helicopter. It was as close a call as I have ever experienced in an aircraft on the ground. It came near washing out the XR-4.

In a way the XR-4 was a flying classroom as well as an engineering laboratory. Several of the officers at Wright Field learned to fly the craft while it was undergoing the various tests. Among these were Colonel Douglas M. Kilpatrick, Colonel P. Ernest Gable, and Major Leslie B. Cooper. On one training flight the XR-4 passed its one hundredth hour in the air, a feat never before accomplished by any helicopter in this country. On this occasion, July 24, 1942, the Commanding General of the Matériel Center, Brigadier General Arthur W. Vanaman, sent a congratulatory wire to Igor Sikorsky:

TODAY THE XR-4 PASSED THE ONE HUNDRED HOUR MARK AND COMPLETED THE PRIMARY TRAINING OF FIVE AIR FORCE OFFICERS TWO OF WHOM SOLOED THIS MORNING. FEW EXPERIMENTAL AIRCRAFT HAVE ACCOMPLISHED SUCH A RECORD IN THE SHORT SPACE OF TWO MONTHS. I EXTEND MY SINCERE CONGRATULATIONS TO YOU AND THE MEMBERS OF YOUR ORGANIZATION WHO TOOK PART IN MAKING THIS POSSIBLE. THE XR-4 IS INDEED PROVING ITS METTLE.

Even those who had been skeptical in the beginning now were forced to admit that the Army's XR-4 was proving successful. No other helicopter had accomplished as much.

Other tests to be conducted involved the use of pontoon-type landing gear. This idea originated at Stratford when the VS-300 performed so efficiently with the rubberized floats in place of its wheels. An order was placed for this type landing gear and,

equipped with it, XR-4, we were certain, could land on practically any kind of surface: the earth, soft, hard, or muddy; pavement, water, ice, or snow. It was a general-purpose landing gear.

By the latter part of August the floats were completed and shipped to Wright Field. They consisted of large rubberized fabric bags. These were inflated with air, giving the XR-4 pontoons. This gave the helicopter a slightly different appearance and it rested much higher off the ground. Unlike the VS-300, which had shock absorbers on its float gear, the XR-4 was minus these protectors, omitted to save weight, and consequently great care had to be exercised until the vibration difficulties, which we knew might be encountered from the whirling rotor, were thoroughly investigated. On the first trial the bags began to dance around on the ground, first on one and then on the other. Never were they high off the ground—no more than fractions of an inch—but they did bounce quite severely. This was whipped by taking off rapidly and positively before the bounce could start. Once the ship was in the air there was still some question as to how the bouncing characteristics would affect it in landings. It was found there was little trouble if the aircraft was positively landed and the rotor not allowed to tarry in coming to a stop.

After landings and take-offs with the floats had been accomplished at the field, the craft was flown to a small pond of water behind the big Huffman Dam near Dayton and a landing on water was executed. The pontoons performed beautifully on the water—there was not the least bit of the bouncing or any other unsatisfactory condition.

Tests were made on Lake Erie. These tests required hovering at various low altitudes over the water. On the day that all equipment was in readiness there was a forty-mile-an-hour wind blowing and the lake was especially rough. It was estimated that the waves were approximately six feet in height. The visibility was poor, and while over the lake there was no horizon, the overcast and the water of the lake seemed to blend together. Under these conditions, flying an airplane without instruments is none too easy; flying a helicopter is even worse. However, the XR-4 did a beautiful job. As it hovered over the waves it gave the impression that it was moving first in one direction and then in the other. Actually it was the water moving beneath, for the craft was standing still. The impression was so marked that it was necessary to tie a small block of wood to a string and drop it from the nose of the XR-4. By keeping this string vertical we were able to hover in relation to the water. No landings were attempted on the lake. We made some, however, in the harbor at Cleveland. Even here the water was choppy. The XR-4 sat down easily and with apparently no disturbance from the waves. Most of these tests were run near the U. S. Coast Guard Station at Cleveland and the men were sincerely interested.

One old watchman, who had seen every type of surface ship, cracked: "I never thought I'd live to see a 'Flying Dutchman,' but danged if that ain't it."

One day after the craft had returned to Wright Field, I was

The Lady seems to hold a YR-4 helicopter.

flying the ship low over the flight line when I got word from the tower that General K. B. Wolfe, Chief of the Production Division, Matériel Center, wanted me to come down at once.

"An important officer wants to see you," said the tower.

It was a great pleasure, for that important officer turned out to be Major General James H. (Jimmy) Doolittle, a friend of mine, fresh back from the Tokyo raid. Short, stocky, bareheaded, grinning Jimmy Doolittle was splitting his sides over that "freakish thing you've been capering around in up there." The helicopter bug had bitten him.

General Wolfe said, "Frank, how about taking Jimmy for a ride?"

"General," I addressed Doolittle, "you may have had quite an experience over Tokyo but this will be one of the tops in your career of flying."

We went for the ride. After a few minutes, I gave the General the controls and let him fly it. He proved himself the master pilot that he is by doing the best job of flying the helicopter of any officer who had even flown it for the first time.

When he came down he was excited about the craft.

"When are we going to get some more?"

I told him others were coming that would be better.

He said then and there he wanted some; that they would be "useful for evacuating the wounded, transporting key personnel, and for supplying isolated units."

"How high will it go?" he asked.

We didn't have the exact data on that, but shortly afterward I began a series of service ceiling tests. For several days in a row we fueled up the XR-4, and I bundled up in flying clothes and off we'd go for a try at a new altitude. Gradually we approached what we thought was the service ceiling, about 11,000 feet. It proved to be more than that, for the ship reached an altitude of over 12,000 feet before its rate of climb declined to one hundred feet a minute, the yardstick that determines an aircraft's service ceiling. At this altitude the craft performed very well except that the control was a little sluggish, but this is true of other aircraft when they reach their service ceiling. Other than this, XR-4 reacted perfectly at the high altitude.

It was a strange feeling being up more than two miles in a helicopter. I had been much higher many times in other aircraft, but this was a feeling that was almost indescribable. More than anything else it was a feeling that you were insecure, like peering down from the Empire State Building. There is a tendency to hang on to something. Up here there was nothing to hang on to. Everything depended upon those rotating blades.

Lieutenant Colonel E. A. Peterman, who watched the climb through powerful glasses, put it this way: "If there are such things as sky hooks, you were hanging from them."

"Pete" was one of the men who helped father the XR-4 at Wright Field. He was observer on most of the test flights. Being a crack engineer, one of the best designers in the business, he made many valuable suggestion concerning the aircraft and helped greatly to expedite the tests. His constant encouragement and reassurance have kept me enthusiastic through some low-ebb minutes with the XR-4 and other helicopters that have since come into being.

By January 5, 1943, the XR-4 had completely finished her tests at Wright Field. Unofficially—only in the sense of the word that there were no members of the official record societies present— the XR-4 broke all world's records for the helicopter. Too, it proved its worth, and on the basis of the test results the Army urged Sikorsky to produce as quickly as possibly the YR-4's, successor models, of which twenty-nine had been ordered. We were going into the vertical-flight business on a big scale.

16
Let's Take a Ride in the XR-4

OVERHEAD THERE IS a clear blue sky. A very gentle, almost negligible summer breeze whispers across the airport. The air is what pilots call a "calm." A brilliant sun hangs in the heavens, sending down rays of moderate temperature. It is the kind of day that God made for the flier. So we are going up in a plane. Not just an ordinary airplane, but a flying machine that will go straight up—a unique contraption that will fly in any of 360 directions. We're going to take a ride in a helicopter.

You and I walk out past the operations office, along behind the rudders of a long line of airplanes that are parked at the edge of the ramp. We're going toward that queer-looking craft at the far end of the line. That's the XR-4. That's the plane in which we're going up to take a look at this world from a perch in the sky. You're going to experience a thrill in flying that you've never had before. You're going to fly so slowly that you'll think you're atop a big building, just looking down. You're going to fly backwards and sideways. Sometimes you're going to feel like you're not flying at all. The helicopter does that to everyone his first time up.

We climb in the transparently inclosed cabin with its side-by-side seats. You enter from the right side. There are two doors. Use the step and, when you sit down, straddle that control stick. That's all right, let it go free between your knees. But don't grab it. Just watch it closely and you'll see how delicately this craft controls.

See those pedals down there at the very bottom of the cabin floor? Those are the rudder pedals. Yes, they do look a little like the clutch and the brake pedal on your car. But they don't do the same thing. Those pedals operate the pitch of the blades on the vertical rotor on the tail. By applying slight pressure to one or the other they vary the angle of pitch of the tail rotor's blades in such a manner as to counteract the torque of the main rotor which is just above your head. See the big blades up there?

Are you comfortable?

Fine. These bucket-type metal seats are not the softest in the world, but then the Army didn't build this machine for a lounge. Maybe when this war is over and you own one of your own there'll be plush-covered seats like you have in your car. But don't worry, if you get uncomfortable just change your position.

It won't upset anything. Sure, go ahead, roll down the glass. It's warm in here and we'll enjoy the ride more.

Now watch closely. See the little handle right here on the floor? That's the gas valve which lets the gasoline flow. On the panel is a booster switch which starts a little electric pump, pressuring the gasoline from the tank to the carburetor. Now we push this little knob forward. The one marked mixture control. It determines the ratio of gasoline and air going to the cylinders. Next we move the clutch handle. That's this lever between the seats here which looks like the emergency brake on your car. It disengages the engine from the rotor and puts a brake on the rotor. Just below this clutch handle is another lever which is called the collective-pitch-control stick. This grip on the end of it is a motorcycle grip-type throttle operated by simply twisting the wrist. A slight turn to the left will open the throttle. Now we raise the safety guard on the starter switch, turn this switch "on," and the engine turns over a couple of revolutions. Hear it? Now to turn the ignition switch on. There she goes. Isn't that a sweet purr? That's the helicopter's heart beating.

The engine is located directly behind us. We twist the grip-type throttle control again to allow the engine to warm up a bit and get it at a desired r.p.m. Look at the instruments on the front panel. There's a tachometer, a fuel gauge, temperature gauge, oil-pressure gauge. Respectively they tell us the speed of the engine in revolutions per minute, how much fuel we have aboard, the oil and cylinder head temperatures, the pressure of the oil going into the engine. By carefully watching them we know just what our engine is doing. That's why they are there.

Everything is running smoothly. The gas pressure is just right. The oil pressure reads properly. So is the temperature okay. The engine is purring. Now I'll reach for the clutch handle and disengage the handle from its locked position by squeezing the spring grip at the top, like releasing the emergency brake in your car. Gradually we allow it to come rearward. As we do this, the clutch begins to engage the gears of the engine with the rotor shaft, starting the rotor blades in rotation. See them slowly turning out there? Let's run the engine and the rotor a minute. Faster. Faster. The rotor blades spin round and round. This is the same as revving the engines on an airplane before take-off.

Close quarters for XR-4 on the Bunker Hill.

We're just getting warmed up.

Look at that little tube that stands upright on top of the instrument panel. That's the rotor pitch indicator—that gadget which looks like a thermometer. It indicates to us the number of degrees of pitch of the blades. Watch it change as we slightly move up on the rotor pitch handle. See? The angle of the blades is changed. We can't see it because they are whirling too fast. But this little instrument tells us that it is changed. And it tells us how much.

The engine is now turning at 2000 r.p.m. That means the blades of the rotor are turning at approximately 215 r.p.m. Don't worry about that vibrating instrument panel up front there. There's nothing wrong with it. The same thing happens in an airplane. And that blue smoke you see coming out from the side. That's just oil burning on the exhaust stack.

Slowly we bring upward the pitch-control handle, which also opens the throttle, since the throttle is synchronized with the pitch-control handle, although it is not a perfect synchronization, and we must open or close the throttle to maintain the desired engine speed. Watch the tachometer. See it climb. We want to hold it at 2150 r.p.m. That's the desired speed. As we apply more power, the torque forces increase. That means we have to push slightly on the left rudder pedal. Like this. This increases the amount of thrust delivered by the tail rotor and keeps the ship from swinging to the right, its normal tendency, because of the rotor turning in the opposite direction.

Notice we haven't moved the stick control. It must be at neutral so that we will take off absolutely vertically from the ground. If it isn't in this position the craft would take off in any one of 360 directions.

The pitch indicator points to nine and a half climbing to ten degrees. That's about right. We have started to create sufficient lift in the blades. Look at the shock struts out there on the landing gear. See them extend? The indicator says ten degrees. We're off!

Straight up she goes. A little noisy maybe, but certainly as vertical as though this thing were an elevator. Still pulling on the pitch-control lever. Increasing the pitch to ten and a half degrees. Up . . . up . . . three . . . four . . . five . . . six feet. Let's hang here for a minute while we decide where we want to go. We push down ever so slightly on the pitch control. The indicator says ten degrees on the dot. Remember we're also decreasing the throttle a little. Likewise the amount of torque decreases. That means we must apply slight pressure to the right rudder, changing the pitch in the vertical rotor in the tail to compensate for this change of torque.

This isn't flying. We're just standing still up here. This is hovering. It is one of the outstanding feats that the helicopter can accomplish which the airplane cannot. Feel the slight shaking. That's because we haven't got the blades perfect yet. But we'll get that someday. Now look at the stick between your knees. See how it moves in a small circle. The stick? The control stick. That's right. Yes, it is a bit noisy. Someday maybe we'll soundproof it more.

Put your hand on the stick and feel the slight movement as I ease it backwards ever so delicately. Feel the tail drop. More pressure backwards on the stick. The tail drops more and the craft is going backwards. Let's go sideways. We move the stick slightly. You can hardly see it or feel it. We drop off to the right side. The more the right side drops, the faster we move in that direction.

We pick up speed going sideways to the right. Since we have a covered tail behind us, the pressure created by movement to the right naturally tends to force the tail over to the left, which means we must apply pressure to the left rudder pedal, increasing the thrust of the tail rotor and pulling the tail of the ship along with us. The tail just sort of tags along with us.

In this maneuver, if we are to stay at our six-foot level it is necessary to increase the pitch slightly, which also opens the throttle a little. The reason for this is more power is required to pull our tail along with us. Want to come back to hovering? Watch. We push slightly on the pitch lever, at the same time moving the control stick to the left. The throttle closes a bit. Naturally, as this is done the torque decreases. So we have to put pressure on the right rudder to keep the tail straight behind us. Now we're hovering again.

Simple, isn't it? All you have to do is think about which way you want it to go and this craft will do it. Anything a horse can do. Want to turn around? All right. We push on the right rudder pedal. Notice the craft turning to the right? The torque force is doing that. We keep the pedal in this position and the ship turns completely around. Like this.

Going up? Gently pull up on the collective-pitch handle. This means increasing the torque so we have to press on the left rudder again. Now we're at twelve feet. We'll return to the six-foot level. Push down on the pitch lever. Take care of the torque reaction with the rudder pedal. Back to six feet. Pull up again on the pitch control. Correct the torque with the rudder pedal. The ship is steady again. Standing still right over the spot we took off from.

So much for vertical flight and backwards and sideways. How about going forward? Slight pressure on the stick forward. This drops the nose of the craft. Feel it? The tail goes up in the air. Look back there and see it suspended. Note the forward motion. More pressure on the stick forward. The nose drops more. We're going faster. It may seem that we are flying along at an angle going down as though we were in a glide. This is not so. See how the ground goes by? We're flying perfectly parallel with it. Sure the nose of the craft is pointed down a little. But that's the way the helicopter flies forward.

In order to stay at six feet we have to decrease the pitch on the main blades. The reason for this is that the rotor moves into undisturbed air and has greater lift, and unless the power and pitch are decreased we may climb. Push the pitch-control lever down. Decrease the amount of torque correction by pushing slightly on the right rudder.

We're gaining speed now. The indicator on the panel in front of us reads forty m.p.h. When we reach that speed and want to go faster at the same altitude we have to increase the main pitch of the blades by pulling up the pitch-control lever. Apply the necessary torque correction by pushing left rudder, since the torque force has been increased with the pitch. There's smooth country ahead, no obstacles, so let's open her up to full speed. We pull up on the pitch control, increasing the pitch of the main rotor, at the same time applying slightly more torque correction in the rudder pedal and still pushing the control stick gently forward. Indicated air speed reads eighty m.p.h., and the aircraft is riding along with its nose at approximately seven degrees down. But we're still flying along comfortably, six feet above the earth. So you see, the helicopter will step out and go, too.

Now we're going to drop from high speed back to cruising speed. But with no change in the altitude. We do three things; watch me. Decrease the pitch of the main blades by pushing the pitch lever down and closing the throttle. Apply pressure on the right rudder pedal, since less torque correction is needed. Simultaneously we pull slightly back on the stick in order to maintain level flight.

We're coming to the end of the smooth stretch now. There are a house and some trees ahead of us. We'd better climb a little. Now we do the same thing we'd do if we were flying an airplane. Open the throttle, which is done by pulling up the pitch lever, pull the stick slightly back, apply rudder correction. There, she lifts prettily, doesn't she? We've climbed a couple hundred feet. The altimeter reads 200 feet. We level off. Set our throttle at cruising, which means we again reduce the pitch of the main blades and apply more pressure on the right rudder pedal. Now we'll bank to the left. See how it's done? Slight movement of the stick to the left. A little left rudder. The craft tilts and swings to the left. We've executed a left bank.

Now you'll agree that we're flying with all responses equivalent to those in a conventional airplane. For instance: when we move the stick slightly to the left instead of flying to the left, we merely bank in that direction. When we pull the stick back, instead of flying backwards the nose merely comes up. We push the stick forward and the nose goes down. But these actions are true only because we are flying forward, in which case this craft is just like an airplane and reacts the same to its controls. Also notice that we have not touched the pitch control, but have maintained the same pitch throughout.

It's nice flying up here, don't you think? You see more than in the airplane. This cabin is like a greenhouse. There is very little to obstruct our vision. We can see above, to either side, and even through the transparent floor. There's your house right down there and just ahead. Land? Sure. How about that spot down in the middle of the block? That's a vacant lot there.

We strike out in a straight line for the landing spot. Here, hold the control stick yourself. Don't put any pressure on it.

Just grip it lightly and get the feel of it. Don't be afraid of it. You can control it with your little finger. See, the movement of the stick is so slight you can hardly feel it at all. Now we're right over the lot. You fly it in. I'll tell you what to do. Decrease the pitch and close the throttle by pushing down on the pitch handle. That's right. Pull back a little on the stick to lift the nose and push gently on the right rudder so we'll adjust for less torque. See what happens? She slows down. Keep your eye on the speed indicator. She's getting below twenty-five m.p.h. Easy, now. Pull up on the pitch-control handle a little. That's right. Now give her a little left rudder for torque correction. We're coming to a stop. More power. Pull up on that pitch-control handle. Remember that increases the throttle, too. She's slipping off to the left. Easy. Give her right rudder and stick. That's it. Now she's stopped. Hold her right here.

We're right over that lot now. Better let me take her in the rest of the way. You observe closely how she reacts. Down slightly on the pitch handle, reducing the pitch, closing the throttle. Pressure on the right rudder for less torque correction. Gently forward on the stick so we can park it right in the center. Still need forward control, you know, to get over the exact spot. We're dropping fast. Down to fifteen feet. We hold the r.p.m. at 2250, which gives us a little excess speed and consequently inertia in the rotor, which we'll use in just a minute. Down to ten feet. We pull up on the pitch lever, increasing the pitch of the blades, opening the throttle, thereby increasing the torque again because the rotor is spinning faster now. Give her a little left rudder. Now we're hovering.

We're going to set her down. Push down on the pitch-control lever, applying more right rudder at the same time to keep our tail straight behind us. She's settling. The wheels touch. There, she's down. Now we push all the way down on the pitch-control handle and let the engine idle. How do you like it?

XR-4 in backward takeoff from deck of Bunker Hill.

XR-4 turns as it takes off.

You're right. It's a wonderful gadget. There are a lot of things that we have to do to this machine before you can take off and land it, although flying it once she is in the air is not very difficult. But then neither is it hard to fly an airplane under those conditions. Naturally, because it will go in so many different directions, the helicopter is harder to fly. Yet, it seems simple enough, doesn't it? Now where to? Back into the air again? Okay.

This time we jump off, go straight up to fifty feet, and then start a gradual climb until we reach 1500 feet. Now I'm going to show you what happens when the engine quits. To simulate this I'm going to push the pitch-control handle down to something under six degrees. Like this. Now the rotor is autorotating. That is, simply by its own gliding motion and the forces acting on its blades the rotor is turning, the same as the rotor on a gyroplane, in autorotation. If you could see it out there, the air has changed its direction. Now it's going up through the rotor instead of coming down through it as was the case when the rotor was under engine power. In this condition there is no torque to counteract because we are in autorotation and descending in a normal glide. We have the same amount of control that we would have in powered flight, with one exception; we must keep descending.

Now let's pull up on the pitch-control lever and engage the blades with the engine again. As we do this we open the throttle and increase the pitch of the main blades, which also increases the amount of torque. That means pressure on the left rudder pedal for counteraction.

Suppose we land without power to prove it can be done. There's the airport over there to the left a little. First we return to autorotative flight. Next, by moving the stick slightly to the left the craft executes a turn in that direction. Notice there is very little noise in the craft now with the motor only idling. Hear the swish of the blades? If they ever stop we're gone ducks. But they won't stop. Notice the wind sock there over the hangar. There's considerably more wind than when we took-off—probably about ten m.p.h. Therefore, even though this is a deadstick landing, a landing without power, we'll head into the wind. The ground is coming up now. We pull back on the stick gently, pulling the nose up. Remember, we're just the same as an airplane, only our glide is steeper and our roll on the ground will be shorter. We're getting close. Watch it. Feel the wheels touch. We roll a little. Not much, but we roll a short distance just as an Autogiro would because, in effect, without our rotor power-driven we are a gyroplane or assume its characteristics at least. There now, are you convinced that we can get down in case of motor failure?

There's the hanger right over there. We'll hop off again and fly low over that line of planes and set her down in front of the hangar doors. This wind blowing will make a slight difference in the craft's performance in the air. When it is hovering, relative to the ground, for instance, it will be flying the speed of the wind. But other than that it will be just the same. Are you ready? All right, let's go. Up on the control-pitch lever. Pressure on the left rudder pedal. Now we're in the air again. We skim over the planes parked in line, come to the spot by the hangar, hover for a minute. We're on the ground again. We disengage the rotor from the engine by pushing forward on the clutch handle and apply the rotor brake by pushing to the forward position. Now, because that wind is blowing it will be necessary to give some thought to stopping the rotor. As the rotor slows down, the centrifugal force becomes less and the blade advancing into the wind will have greater lift. Therefore, we must hold the control stick in a position such that the pitch of the blade is decreased as it makes its advance, so it will not lift. Otherwise the wind would lift the blade and when it reached the other side of its cycle it would fall down and possibly damage the tail of the craft, the blade, or both.

We snap off the gas. The engine stops. We turn off the ignition switch, snap off the other electrical switches. Our flight is done.

You've flown in the XR-4.

Continuing the turn in takeoff from Bunker Hill.

17
The Bunker Hill

NAMED FOR THE HEROES who fought and died on the slopes of Bunker Hill in the Revolutionary War, the War Shipping Administration's tanker, S. S. *Bunker Hill*, was helping to preserve the freedom they won. She helped fight and win the Battle of the Atlantic. In her hull millions of gallons of precious gasoline crossed the ocean to feed the planes and tanks that smashed at our enemy. Now, her hold empty of its explosive cargo, a superstructure atop her deck amidships, she was out to make history. For the first time a helicopter was going to land on the deck of a ship—slip cautiously through her maze of rigging and masts and come to a stop right below the pilothouse. The *Bunker Hill* was to take part in a revolutionary experiment that might help decide the war, at least provide a new kind of protection for the all-important convoys.

The demonstration took place on May 6 and 7 of 1943, on Long Island Sound, under the joint auspices of the Army Air Forces, the Maritime Commission, and the War Shipping Administration. It was held for one purpose and that purpose only: to prove the practicability of a helicopter landing on a small deck of a tanker. If successful, in all probability it meant individual air protection for our tankers and Liberty Ships plying the dangerous waters of the Atlantic in the biggest and most vital supply line known to the world.

The spring of '43 was like a field day for the Axis submarines. The prowlers of the deep took a savage toll of U. S. and Allied ships carrying the balance of power to Britain. Even Henry J. Kaiser and his ship-a-day methods couldn't keep up with the sinkings. The situation was gravely serious. Some of the once white-sand beaches along our Eastern coastline were black with the oil and gasoline that should have been in the wing tank of a bomber or in the gears of a half-track. In desperation we turned to any new idea that seemed a plausible way to beat off the subs. How about the helicopter?

To get the answer, I went to Stratford to fly the XR-4 in a series of tests—landings and take-offs from the deck of the tanker *Bunker Hill*—which, it was believed, would, once and for all, settle the question as to whether the straight-up-and-down aircraft could operate efficiently from the deck of an ordinary freighter.

When I first saw the XR-4 on this occasion, as Les Morris and I walked out of the Sikorsky factory to the aircraft, she looked all dressed up in her go-to-meetin' clothes. Her aluminum paint job glistened in the sun's rays. She had a new set of rotor blades that were slightly longer than the others and she had a new engine which was more powerful than the one installed while she was at Wright Field. She again had donned her all-purpose landing gear—a big pair of rubberized floats thirty inches in diameter and thirteen feet in length which looked like a couple of oversized hot dogs.

These floats, Les Morris told me, had caused him considerable worry. In test trials with the craft, to make sure she was ready for the tanker demonstration, he had noticed that there was an overamount of bouncing when he landed. Hoping to stop this condition, he had devised a unique shock-chord arrangement around the struts that held the floats. For stability of the pontoons two pieces of two-by-four planking as crossbars had been fastened to the floats. It made the ship, which otherwise was in spick-and-span condition, look as though she were wearing a pair of old work shoes. Frankly, although Les doesn't agree with me on this, I don't think the idea made much difference on the bouncing. XR-4 still bounced a bit when I landed her.

While we were making this last-minute inspection of the ship, Les stopped me for a minute and pointed toward the Sound, where the *Bunker Hill* lay at anchor.

"See that little pilothouse there amidships?" he pointed.

I nodded.

"Now see that mast a few feet the other side of it?" Les continued.

"Sure."

"Well, Colonel, in between those two you're going to land the XR-4."

"Are you kidding?" I asked him. "You mean somebody else is going to land in that space—not me. Why, Les, there isn't room enough for the helicopter to land between that structure and the rear mast—at least, it doesn't look that way."

Les reassured me. He pointed out that the normal cargo deck of the tanker offered a space of 78 by 60 feet for a landing area. Immediately aft of this space were mast and stays. Ahead were housing structures. The only clear approach to the landing area was from either side. It was easy to determine the rest. If the XR-4 were sitting in the center of that space with its nose pointed toward the bow of the ship, there would be a fourteen-foot clearance at each end—fourteen feet from the mast and a like distance from the pilothouse. That wasn't much leevway for a flying machine. It recalled the days at Wright Field during the early tests when we had landed on that twenty-foot-square platform, though we had clear approaches to it. The practice would come in handy now.

Actually there was painted on the deck of the *Bunker Hill* a fifty-foot square with an eight-foot bull's-eye in the center. Landing right smack in the center of the bull's-eye, the XR-4, with her thirty-eight-foot diameter rotor and a tail rotor which extended some twelve feet beyond that, would take up nearly all of this space. What was left over you had to measure in pilot skill.

There was no doubt about it, this would be tough. If the landing area were on the stern of the boat it wouldn't be so bad. That way there would be plenty of space to use in case the approach wasn't just right. You could back up or go to either side. The *Bunker Hill* didn't offer that freedom. There was only one way to approach her for a landing—that was side-on. And there was only one way to go if the first try wasn't just right—the same way you had come in. But we knew one thing, that if the helicopter could do the job under these conditions, it would be comparatively simple to change the location of the landing deck to the stern of a ship. In fact, we were already formulating plans for such tests.

Long Island Sound was very tranquil. The waters spread out like a big sheet of plate glass. A bright sun beat down and the sky had little patches of white wispy clouds. It was an ideal day as I pointed the nose of the XR-4 away from the factory and out toward the big tanker. There was no wind and that meant approaches could be made from either side of the ship.

When the XR-4 eased over the ship, the space on the deck looked even smaller than it did when I viewed the *Bunker Hill* from off shore. It didn't look at all as if the helicopter would fit. The cabin superstructure towered up like a big two-story building, and the people on it all had that "it can't be done" look on their faces. On the other side the rear mast tapered skyward with its heavy cable guy wires fanning out to make the landing even more hazardous. Yet that big white bull's-eye stuck out like a target challenging a marksman, and if the measurements were correct, it could be done.

The helicopter hovered over the ship for a minute, made a complete circle, and came back, approaching from the port side for a landing. Nose first it came in, stopping about forty feet above the deck and the same distance away from the ship. Then at a forty-five-degree angle it descended with the bull's-eye centered in the glass windows of the cabin floor. It was not an absolutely vertical descent, but the XR-4 came true to the white marker as though being pulled by a powerful magnet, and a minute later the floats touched the deck. She shook a little and then relaxed, her fuselage covering the white center. A helicopter, for the first time ever, had landed on the deck of a freighter. I disengaged her rotor, shut off the engine, and she eased back on her haunches, satisfied and pleased.

Only the first phase, however, had been accomplished. It was all well and good to make a landing on the deck of the tanker when it was anchored only a few miles off shore. But how about landing when the ship was under way, cutting through the water at several knots' speed? How about landing when there was a wind? These things were still untried. And unless they could be accomplished, the whole idea was just so much rotor-wash. Consequently, XR-4 had barely come to rest before the ship hoisted anchor and her turbines put her in motion. A couple of small Coast Guard cutters escorted us—one of the precautions taken for safety. It was a good feeling having them near by in case of any mishap.

At five knots' speed, the vessel's movement was barely negligible and the XR-4 got off as though she were taking to the air from that platform back at Wright Field. I flew out over the water a few hundred yards, hovered over the stern of one of the cutters, and then returned to negotiate the first landing while the *Bunker Hill* was in motion. The speed was so slow that it was little different and no trickier than landing when the vessel was standing still.

But one lesson was learned which undoubtedly helped along the success of the tests that were to follow. It was impossible to see the mast and stays which were behind the XR-4, near the tail rotor, as the helicopter made its approach. After the first landing it was estimated that if the nose edge of the floats was always on the white line running across the deck, one side of the square, the main rotor blades had six feet clearance in front and there was, of course, ample tail clearance. It was a comforting thought, a sort of a guide to go by that helped immensely in making all landings. To the pilot it was a big safety factor that relieved, to a slight degree, the tense, ever-present element of danger. But to those who watched the whole demonstration from the two-story bridge it presented a new mental hazard. The whirling blades of the rotor cut through the air only a few feet

Visitors on Bunker Hill *inspect XR-4 after flight demonstration.*

from where they were standing and in precisely the same plane. If they should come more than six feet closer it might decapitate nervous spectators.

The speed of the tanker was increased to seven and one-half knots. More take-offs and landings were negotiated, the helicopter making its approaches from both sides of the ship. Since there was little noticeable difference in the difficulties of landing or taking off at this speed, the tanker pushed her forward motion to ten, then fifteen knots, finally pouring out her full speed and leaving a wake behind that rolled the small cutters following her.

As the freighter increased her speed, the landings became more and more difficult. Chiefly this was due to the turbulent air that swept down off the superstructure and made the landing-deck area a series of burbling air currents. Whenever the XR-4 came in for hovering, preparatory to setting her floats down, the craft bounced about, and with the narrow clearances, it was plenty tricky to negotiate a landing. Sometimes the XR-4 bounced a bit when she touched the deck, and to say that the pilot was not too sure of himself would be putting it mildly. Those on deck who were watching Sikorsky said that the XR-4's designer tried to fly the helicopter, during the landings, himself, going through the motions like a man trying to win on a pin-ball machine. A total of about twelve landings was accomplished the first day, and then the helicopter was flown back to the factory. The next day we were going to put on a demonstration for high government officials.

A thick fog hung over Stratford on the morning of May 7 and you couldn't see the tanker from the factory yard. The demonstration was scheduled to start at ten-thirty and, a quarter of an hour before, the visibility was less than two miles and a gentle breeze was blowing. But since the helicopter could practically "feel" its way, I took off and headed out over the Sound in the general direction of the spot where the *Bunker Hill* had come to anchor the night before. In a few short minutes the shape of the tanker came up out of the fog and as the helicopter came nearer and nearer it was even possible to ascertain the sizable crowd that lined her bridge, all waiting for the show to begin. I thought it would be a good idea to show them how gentle the XR-4 could set down on the water. So, after circling the ship once, the helicopter was landed on the smooth surface of the Sound a few hundred feet away from the tanker. The "hot dog" floats settled into the almost glassy waters with little more than a ripple. Then the engine roared again and the craft lifted herself as smoothly as she had landed, the blast from her rotor going downward and eddying the water below.

Once more XR-4 circled the *Bunker Hill* and then approached for her landing. On deck there was plenty of excitement. Seamen ran to and fro, making sure that everyone and everything was out of the landing area. Others stood by with emergency equipment in case the helicopter might hit something and crash. The little bridgelike affair around the pilothouse was lined with crew members, officers, and dignitaries of the government agencies who

Igor Sikorsky, Frank Gregory, Richard W. Seabury, Stanley V. Parker, and Gover Loening discuss potentials.

were there to witness the unusual feat. Richard W. Seabury of the War Shipping Administration, Brigadier General John W. Franklin of the Army Transportation Corps, Admiral Stanley V. Parker of the U. S. Coast Guard, and Grover Loening, one of aviation's notables, were on hand. But the two men whose eyes never left the XR-4 for an instant, whose minds and muscles were living every second of the landing, were Les Morris and Igor Sikorsky. It was a big day, especially for Sikorsky. Another one of those "dream ideas" of his had become a reality. The helicopter was landed on the white bull's-eye with its nose headed to starboard and the tail to port.

The ship was going at approximately fifteen knots. The wind at this particular time was coming approximately twenty degrees from the portside, which meant that if a take-off were made in the direction the craft was headed, turbulence and downdraft would make the maneuver extremely hazardous. Consequently, when the XR-4 took off for the first time on the demonstration, she hovered a few feet above the deck, turned approximately one hundred and fifty degrees to the left, then stuck her nose down a little and went forward smack into the wind.

During the remainder of the day, take-offs and landings were made from every direction, with the ship going downwind, into the wind, crosswind, and at various speeds, to show that the helicopter could be landed under almost any condition.

Late in the afternoon Colonel R. C. Wilson, Chief of the Development Branch, Matériel Division, Office of the Assistant Chief of Air Staff for Matériel, Maintenance, and Distribution, in Washington, D. C., climbed into the other seat of the XR-4. It was urgent that he be in Washington within a few hours. His plane was at the Stratford airport. Thus he became the first ship-to-shore passenger in the helicopter—the first helicopter taxi service in the world. The XR-4 landed him at the administration building at the airport in a short time. His passenger to Washington was Lieutenant Colonel Allan P. Tappan, who also used the helicopter taxi. Then the helicopter returned to the *Bunker Hill* and took other members of the official party ashore to the field at the Sikorsky plant.

The demonstration was over.

A few days later Rear Admiral Howard L. Vickery, Vice-Chairman of the Maritime Commission and Deputy War Shipping Administrator, after reviewing reports from the officials who had seen the demonstration, issued this statement:

"Under the circumstances existing at the time of the demonstration of helicopters' ability to take off and land on the deck of tankers, the United States Maritime Commission and the War Shipping Administration believe that the feasibility of the operation has been sufficiently proved. These agencies are now preparing a plan for a small deck to be installed on Liberty Ships without interfering with the cargo arrangement which will permit helicopters to be used at sea, thus giving the ships added protection against submarines."

To those of us who were close to the problem, we knew that the *Bunker Hill* was merely a practice test. The ship, empty and operating in the seldom rough waters of Long Island Sound, could not be likened to landings aboard a ship heavily laden with cargo and plowing through the rolling surface of the Atlantic. The preliminary evidence was good, however. In order to be certain that operations from the decks of seagoing ships would be practicable, there was but one thing left to do—try the same tests under actual conditions. The *Bunker Hill* had served its purpose. We had proved that the helicopter could operate from the deck of a merchant ship. We, however, were more convinced than ever that the best location for the landing deck would be on the stern of the ship. In the not-too-distant future we were to have an opportunity to test our conclusion.

18
We Fly the Mail

THE FIRST REGULAR civilian air mail in the world began on May 15, 1918, when U. S. Army Air Service pilots, flying in old JN-1 training biplanes (the popular "Jenny"), carried pouches filled with letters from New York to Washington.

Lieutenant Torrey H. Webb took off from Hazelhurst Field (now a part of Roosevelt Field, Long Island) and headed south, landing at Philadelphia, where Lieutenant J. C. Edgerton took over the controls and flew the mail on to Washington. At the airport the bags were transferred to a fast mail truck and rushed to the Capitol, the destination of most of the correspondence.

Twenty-five years later, on May 16, 1943, the helicopter took off from the Capitol terrace and delivered some rush mail to a waiting airliner at the Washington municipal airport as part of a nation-wide celebration program heralding the quarter-century mark of the air-mail service. That helicopter was the YR-4, first of the service-test models of the Army-Sikorsky helicopter to be delivered.

A few days before, Major Leslie B. Cooper (now Lieutenant Colonel) and the author left Wright Field for the Sikorsky plant in Connecticut. We found two helicopters in the air at the same time as we approached the field. Les Morris was flying the new YR-4 and another Sikorsky test pilot, Jimmy Viner, was flying the XR-4, which had been returned to the company for further testing after we had "wrung it out" at Wright Field. It was the first time in this country and, as far as we knew, the first time in the world that two helicopters of basically the same design were in the air at the same time.

From all outside appearances the YR-4 looked like an exact replica of the first Army-Sikorsky machine. Certainly its configuration was the same. But there were some changes that are worth-while noting here.

The exhaust pipe, which came out of the side, had its opening upward instead of coming through the bottom as was the case with the X machine. This threw the exhaust up and out into the air, which was an improvement, since the helicopter, as it came near the earth and hovered, could not now set fire to a grassy field or other inflammable materials with flame from its exhaust stacks.

The "dome" on the back of the XR-4 which housed the support for the rotor shaft was heightened on the new helicopter, thus placing the top of it closer to the plane of the rotor.

Location of the tail wheel, which hung down on a frame under the tail of the XR-4, was moved farther back on the Y model to protect the tail rotor in case of an autorotative landing.

On the XR-4, cooling air for the engine came in from the tail, while in the YR-4 the air entered through an opening in the "dome" on top. This change was also made on the XR-4.

The engine installed in the YR-4 was a 180-horsepower Warner seven-cylinder, air-cooled engine, whereas in the first Army ship there was a 165-horsepower engine of the same basic design. This higher-powered engine was also installed in the XR-4 after her return to the factory.

Rotor blades on the YR-4 were increased one foot in length, from eighteen feet to nineteen feet, making the diameter of the rotor thirty-eight feet instead of thirty-six feet. These longer blades were also installed on the XR-4.

Radio communication equipment was installed in the YR-4. The XR-4 had no means of communicating with the ground while in flight.

An increase of five gallons' capacity for the YR-4's tank over the XR-4 was made. Both burned 78 octane gasoline.

These were the chief differences.

Our job was to get these two helicopters and fly them to Fort Monmouth, New Jersey, for tests with the Signal Corps. The mission was to be twofold, for after the military application tests we were to proceed to Washington, D. C., and participate in the air-mail-anniversary celebration. At long last, the close-mouthed references to the Army's helicopter could come out in the open. We were going to show the public our latest development in helicopters and put on a history-making demonstration right in front of the Capitol. By this time most people knew that the Army had a successful helicopter, but few had seen any practical demonstrations with it.

The distance from the Sikorsky plant in Stratford to Fort Monmouth is approximately one hundred miles. It was decided that Major Cooper would fly the XR-4 and I would fly the new job in "mass" formation from the factory to our destination. A factory representative, again Adolph Plenefisch, was to accompany me on the trip, while Les Cooper would fly alone with our baggage. That was a wise move because the Major weighs 240 pounds and can just cram his long legs into the cabin of the helicopter. He says then they still stick out.

Up around Stratford by this time, the people were accustomed to seeing helicopters. They started to predict the weather by them. Some seemed to think that, when one of Sikorsky's "whirling bugs" did not fly around the sky sometime during the day, there was fierce weather coming and everyone had better take cover. Two of the Army-Sikorsky helicopters in the air at the same time, though, was an event.

It was a beautiful clear May morning when we took off, and both of the helicopters got into the air as smoothly as a professional swimmer leaves the diving board and with about as much grace. First the XR-4, then the YR-4 which followed her in quick succession, maintaining a position behind and above Cooper's ship. Through the glass bottom I could see a big broad grin on Sikorsky's face as he talked to Les Morris and made sweeping gestures with his arms at his "two babies" flying up there like a couple of hummingbirds.

We headed out over the Housatonic River, leaving the immediate vicinity of the factory and cruising south down the coastline of Connecticut. After a little while Major Cooper let the XR-4 drop back to what would normally be a wing position in a formation, permitting the YR-4 to take the lead and do the navigating.

We gently and gracefully made our way along the edge of Long Island Sound and then decided to streak out and fly across this small body of water over to Long Island. It was probably the longest overwater flight ever attempted to that date with the helicopter. My passenger frowned and made the remark that it would be "just too bad if the engine should quit." Actually the worst that could have happened would have been a good ducking, but the cold gray waters of the Sound didn't look inviting for a swim.

From out of nowhere a huge flying boat cut across in front of us. It was the Atlantic Clipper, probably just heading in from a European crossing. Someday, we thought, the helicopter may too be a commercial carrier. As the shoreline of Coney Island spread itself out below us, Plenefisch and I both exchanged prognostications about the day when the bathers who flocked there in the summer months would probably fly down in their helicopters. Then we laughed at our futuristic dream because we both knew anybody who would own a helicopter would hop away from this crowd and fly to a nice quiet beach somewhere south or north along the great Atlantic shoreline.

The entire trip from Stratford to Fort Monmouth took us about an hour and thirty minutes. As we came in over the military post, both helicopters circled the Headquarters Building, and down on the ground we could see many uniformed personnel heading out toward the parade ground where they anticipated we would land.

The temptation was too great. There in front of the administration building was a small triangular-shaped lawn. There were some trees around the perimeter and a couple more shaded the middle area around the flagpole that towered up directly in front of the building's entrance, with Old Glory whipping in the light breeze.

Why not land her right in the middle down there?

"Do it," urged Plenefisch.

Land her we did, and the YR-4 halted about fifty feet above the ground and then settled, gentle as a feather, right at the base of the flagpole, a few feet away from the front door of headquarters.

An officer out of breath came up to the ship and panted: "You sure surprised us. We thought you would land on the parade ground. Never expected this."

A few minutes later the post's commandant came out and said jokingly: "What's the idea, Colonel, of making my front lawn into a landing field?"

Major Cooper in the meantime had landed on the baseball diamond which was at one corner of the parade ground.

There was considerable talk about the two helicopters that night. Many were confused about the color schemes on the two craft. The YR-4 was camouflaged with olive-drab fuselage and rotor and battleship gray on its underside, while the XR-4 was still finished in aluminum. One of the ladies remarked at the officer's club that evening: "I saw the helicopters come in and noticed that the Army landed on the front lawn but the Navy landed in the back on the parade ground."

We called Major Cooper "Admiral" from then on.

The next day we made several flights, including taking the commanding general from his office building to his quarters and returning. Then some tests were run with the Signal Corps in the calibration of radar equipment. Since the helicopter could hover still in one spot, it was comparatively simple for the men on the ground to train the equipment on the ship and make any calibrations they desired.

While at Fort Monmouth we also ran some test missions in the field with an infantry company. The men were well hidden

Igor Sikorsky and Frank Gregory observe the close quarters for operations.

YR-4 heads for the James Parker.

in an encampment in a thick wood, and we flew their commanding officer from heaquarters to his camp site and sat him down right among the tall trees where there was a small clearing no more than 150 feet square. The boys were very much amazed. This was the first time a helicopter in free flight ever had been used on a military mission, though the whole thing was purposely staged and certainly was under no battle conditions.

These and other tests behind us, we proceeded to Washington in order to be there on the 16th for the air-mail-anniversary celebration. Both the helicopters were in the air again and we started cross-country. This was, indeed, quite an experience, flying cross-country at sixty-five or seventy m.p.h., especially when I have had the pleasure of flying at 300 miles an hour and more. The helicopter had great promise for the tourist who wanted to see the countryside. It seemed that we would hover for several minutes over a check point before continuing on. Now I could appreciate Les Morris' enthusiasm over his flight in the XR-4. This was really fun, though I had to admit we weren't getting places very fast.

Our course took us over the Platt-LePage Aircraft plant at Eddystone, Pennsylvania, and as we approached the vicinity of the plant we noticed a craft, not too strange, flying in the air below us. It was the XR-1, the Army's second helicopter, the twin-rotor craft, on a test flight. Lou Leavitt was at its controls. Once again I couldn't resist temptation. I hadn't intended making a stop at Eddystone. We left our course, began losing altitude, and settled down to landings in the field adjacent to the Baldwin Locomotive Works beside the XR-1. Three helicopters in one field—another first.

The whole Platt-LePage plant, it seemed, turned out to see the two visiting craft. Even Laurence LePage and Hal Platt were there and much was said in the way of comparing the XR-1 with the R-4 ships. LePage informed us that the tests with the XR-1 were progressing, but the craft still wasn't over its teething troubles. As yet no closed-course flight had been made with the ship, although it had been in the air many times.

"We'll make it soon," he assured us.

A few days later he made good his word. Early in June I flew the ship on its first closed-circuit flight. Unfortunately, on July 4 it suffered an accident which did considerable damage, described in an earlier chapter. When we saw her in May she looked mighty prim.

From Eddystone we continued on our way to the capital, flying via Wilmington, Delaware, and then on to the National Airport at Washington, D. C., where my good friend Ed Frohlich of the Borg-Warner Corporation, builders of some of the component parts of the YR-4, was there to meet us. The next morning we were due at the Capitol at 9:30 A.M. to pick up a parcel of letters from the Speaker of the House, Sam Rayburn, for "rush" delivery to the airport and thence out by regular air transport—the first planned air-mail delivery made by a helicopter.

The next morning the weather was practically zero-zero.

There was a slow drizzle. Looking up was like glancing at a gray sheet. We took a taxi to the airport and when we walked in to the operations office the CAA man on duty there quipped: "You aren't flying today. Why, man, even the birds are walking." He evidently wasn't familiar with the helicopter.

The visibility was actually one-eighth of a mile, and the ceiling was practically on the ground. It took some "hot" convincing before the CAA inspector would let me take the YR-4 off the ground. I told him that the helicopter could make its way through the fog the same way as an automobile and that there were plenty of people driving their cars to work that morning, including, most likely, Congressman Rayburn, who would be mighty disappointed if that helicopter didn't show up at the Capitol at the appointed time. Finally he agreed, and after a final check to make sure everything was in good working order I took off in the YR-4 and headed for the Capitol building.

Halfway across the field, and the administration building was enveloped in the fog. It just vanished from sight. This was murky weather. Nobody but a fool or a helicopter pilot would fly in anything like this. We were inching our way. Literally feeling our way above the ground. Airport, runways, boundary lights, the edge of the field, finally the Potomac River was directly beneath the ship. I crossed the Potomac to the east bank, then followed its shoreline to the Anacostia River, then up the Anacostia to the Eleventh Street Bridge. It was difficult to see far ahead. Only by straining, it seemed, was it possible to make out the landmarks so clothed in still, mysterious, gray fog, so thick that the rotor blades seemed to slice through it, leaving a pathway in the air.

Now I was flying so low up Eleventh Street that driving a car wouldn't have been much closer to the ground. Pennsylvania Avenue came underneath and I turned to the left, knowing that ahead in this fog was the Capitol. I was anxious to know just how good the visibility was, so I kept a keen eye open for the Capitol dome. At first glimpse of it, I would count the blocks. Soon, I thought I saw it towering through the mist. One, two, three—three blocks' visibility. I was wrong. That was the dome of the Library of Congress building, an indication of the type of visibility at three blocks. But right ahead was the Capitol dome, and I eased the YR-4 to a dead-stop landing on the pavement right in front of the building steps. It was 9:15, a quarter of an hour ahead of schedule.

There was a small group of spectators with their umbrellas and raincoats to protect them from the light drizzle. News photographers flashed their cameras, and I made a quick take-off and put the ship through some antics—backwards, sideways, and so on—for movie cameramen; then sat her back down again.

Congressman Rayburn was there precisely at 9:30 and witnessed a like demonstration; then, without bringing the craft to an actual landing, I hovered about a foot off the ground and Mr. Rayburn came over, with a pleasant smile, and handed me the little brown Manila folder containing the letters.

Within five minutes the letters were in the dispatchers' office

YR-4 above the deck of the James Parker.

YR-4 takes off in moderately rough seas.

YR-4 proves the water a good place to land too.

Frank Gregory on his way up by rescue hoist.

Frank Gregory reaches for the floor.

Safe aboard after being hoisted from the ground.

at the airport. The helicopter, for the first time in history, had carried the mail.

That afternoon the weather had cleared, and the XR-4 and the YR-4 put on a public demonstration at the national airport for all to see. The YR-4 at one time hovered about a foot above the ground and took on a passenger, made a short flight, and let him disembark the same way. Then I let the ship hover about thirty feet in the air while my passenger lowered a rope and descended to the ground. He said later he didn't like the trick, however, because he burned his hand a little sliding down the Manila strands.

During these demonstrations a direct-control Autogiro flown by John M. Miller of Eastern Airlines circled overhead. It was the KD-1 built and owned by the Kellett Aircraft Corporation, the original prototype of the YG-1s, and there were many individuals who, seeing the three rotary-wing aircraft in the air at the same time, thought they were witnessing the flight of three helicopters. I wished then that I could have explained to them the difference.

The following day both Les Cooper and I departed in the two helicopters for Philadelphia and from there made the 140-mile flight to the Sikorsky factory in Stratford—the longest nonstop flight on record for any helicopter.

The Army's helicopters had proved their prowess.

19
The James Parker

BEHIND THE CLOSED doors of an office in The Pentagon in Washington, D. C., where our military leaders plan the strategy of global war, a strange venture was being formulated. Two men were present, Brigadier General John W. Franklin of the Army Transportation Corps and the author. Until recently what we talked about was secret. Now it can be told. We were discussing plans for a helicopter demonstration aboard a fast troop transport to prove the feasibility of using the helicopter as added air protection for individual ships that plied the ocean paths.

Tall, slim, deep-voiced General Franklin, who was president of one of the nation's foremost steamship lines before he donned a uniform, was eager for the experiment to get under way. "Gregory," he said, "everything has been approved for the tests with the James Parker. We can go ahead as soon as the preparations are completed."

The James Parker was a troop ship, a luxury liner before the war. Now she had her innards torn out. Swinging hammocks, one above the other, hung from her interior structural members which once supported dining tables and the fixtures to make up a modern salon. Her sides, once white, were now a musty gray, and the slime of the sea clung to her dull-colored hull.

General Franklin told me this and he knew the Parker, for a photograph of a sister ship, bedecked with ribbons and brilliantly painted, hung on the wall behind his desk. He knew, too, the vital importance of keeping such ships afloat, guarding them against the enemies that prowled the deep. The thousands of soldiers they could carry across the ocean in one sailing could turn the tide of a beachhead where the fighting was toughest. The Army Transportation Corps was charged with getting them there, and safely. That's why General Franklin and his associates, fulfilling their responsibility to the best of their know-how, were anxious to try the helicopter, for in this rotary-wing aircraft they saw a new "pair of eyes" for their troop ships. Saw in this craft the one way to prevent their fast troop carriers from getting into a position for a submarine to fire its torpedoes—spot it before the ship could get near enough for the sub to launch an attack.

The fast ships seldom travel in convoy, seldom are escorted at all. They go it alone. Their protection is their speed. Ships like the Queen Mary, the Queen Elizabeth, the America, and others which once made record crossings of the Atlantic were built for speed and luxury. Every maiden voyage was a race for the blue-ribbon crossing—the Bremen, the Rex, the Normandie, the two Queens; each won the coveted honor when they were making scheduled crossings, carrying tourists and mail during the days of peace. It is generally conceded that such ships are faster than any submarine, therefore, to be a real danger a sub must come upon them at just the right instant from just the right angle in order to let go its potential death. This has happened in this war when a big British liner went down, victim of a sub's torpedoes. To guard against that one chance, the idea of carrying aircraft to patrol the area ahead of the ship was conceived. The helicopter was seen as ideal for the job.

It was agreed that the helicopter is no adequate substitute for the usual antisubmarine aircraft. Therefore, if aircraft from land bases can be utilized in escorting a given convoy or if aircraft from a carrier can be so utilized, the usefulness of the helicopter as an additional protector is quite problematical. The helicopter should be used for convoys where air coverage is impossible and for independent high-speed vessels only.

In order to be effective against the submarine menace the helicopter should be able to produce a sufficient volume of fire at the sub so as to force at least some of the submarines (if in a pack) to submerge and perhaps even damage some of them, which probably could be done by installing forward-firing rocket weapons.

The general duty of the helicopter would be to perform the general escort coverage sweep around a convoy, looking for submarines at distances of from ten to twenty miles from the convoy. The helicopter thus could spot an enemy sub and relay the location of it to surface vessels which could hunt it down.

It was in June of 1943 that I had the talk with General Franklin. Leaving his office, I went to New York, where the James Parker in dock was being fitted with a specially constructed deck atop its stern to accommodate a helicopter and allow for vertical-flight operations. Colonel J. H. Holder of the Port of Embarkation was in charge of the construction work, and his men already had part of the structure completed. It was to be a deck forty-by-forty-foot square, built as a superstructure over the stern. This location, we had learned from tests on the tanker Bunker Hill, was most desirable.

Holder and his men had worked hard to get the ship ready. When I first saw the deck framework—the planking was not yet down—I knew the area was not too small, but incorrectly positioned. Two large king posts used for crane and hoist operations in loading the transport butted the forward end of the proposed deck space. This meant that the helicopter's rotor would have no clearance and consequently, since the forward side of the original forty-by-forty square was walled in by the king posts, it limited the space of operation to a twenty-by-forty-foot rectangle. The only solution was to lengthen the platform by extending it twenty feet toward the stern of the vessel. Colonel Holder assured me that the situation would be remedied and that the deck planking would be in place so that we could start the tests in about ten days. That gave me just time enough to go to the Sikorsky factory to check final preparation on the aircraft.

We were going to use the two helicopters that had visited Washington, D. C., in May for these landing and take-off trials. Both the XR-4 and the YR-4 were to take part in the experiment. Getting ready was a big task. Besides the author, three other Wright Field officers—Lieutenant Colonel Leslie B. Cooper and Lieutenants Harold H. Hermes and Frank W. Peterson—were engaged in the preparation of the helicopters. The two latter officers had just finished their training at the Sikorsky factory and both were to fly the ships during the experiments. There was a long list of things to do. First we had to check and double check the aircraft themselves, for this was the first time that a helicopter was to venture out to sea. We didn't want to take any chances of failures. To protect the craft from salt-water spray, special covers were cut and sewed from canvas cloth. Special stiltlike frames were designed and built to aid in securing the helicopters to the deck, for we knew that the *Parker* would be at sea for at least a couple of days, and no one could predict what kind of weather we should run into. Then there was the matter of getting sufficient gasoline and oil aboard for approximately twenty hours' flying time. All of this was the Army's responsibility; specifically seeing that it was done and done properly was my job. The contractor's personnel co-operated one hundred per cent, which was characteristic of their support.

In addition to these general problems we had to fit the floats onto the YR-4, since it was decided the newer craft would operate with floats and the XR-4 would have conventional wheeled landing gear. Colonel Cooper was to fly the XR-4 aboard and Lieutenant Frank W. Peterson was to fly the YR-4.

Trouble at Stratford broke from an unexpected quarter. An unfortunate accident occurred which threatened to ground all helicopters, including the XR-4 and the YR-4. This would have halted the tests before they even began. Commander Frank Erickson of the U. S. Coast Guard, flying in a second YR-4, had one of the blades on the tail rotor get out of line and strike the framework which supports the tail rotor. Luckily, the craft was only a few feet off the ground and the Commander was able to land immediately. All that was needed was to repair the frame-

work and replace the rotor. Considerable thought was given as to whether or not there was sufficient clearance between the blades and the frame. Engineers immediately, to avoid further hazards, wanted to ground all the helicopters until more clearance was provided. Close inspection revealed that a blade stop was worn sufficiently to permit the blade to leave its normal plane of rotation. Although in future models the clearance was increased, the stops were inspected on the XR-4 and the YR-4 and the original plans were followed for the ship-landing demonstration. We called the accident an isolated case. Splendid records with the other helicopters substantiated our decision of ordering the tests to continue as scheduled.

The day after Independence Day, 1943, two strange-looking aircraft appeared over New York Harbor. Both Cooper and Peterson were right on schedule, and after hovering over the harbor for a few minutes they brought the XR-4 and the YR-4 to rest on the specially prepared deck of the *James Parker*, which was moored at one of the docks along the water front. The XR-4 came in first and was quickly pushed to one side as the second helicopter settled to the deck. This was the first time that two such craft had ever landed in so small a space, including all ground operations.

The following day, about noon, the troop ship weighed anchor and moved out into the mouth of the Hudson. While the small tugs heaved and chugged as they pulled her to open water, the two helicopters buzzed up and down, making numerous practice landings on the ship's afterdeck structure. Since the three Army pilots and Les Morris had had no experience in landing aboardship, the *James Parker* was brought to anchor again in the harbor and the take-offs and landings continued with each pilot having his turn at the fun. That night a little flotilla of small motorboats began to bring personages aboard who were to witness the tests. Among these were: Brigadier General John W. Franklin, Brigadier General Benjamin W. Chidlaw, Colonel E. E. Aldrin of the first Sea-Search Attack Group, Langley Field, Virginia, Colonel Erik H. Nelson from Headquarters Army Air Forces, Commander James S. Russell, representing the Navy, and Wing Commander R. A. C. Brie, Royal Air Force, of the British Air Commission. Others present included Richard W. Seabury of the War Shipping Administration, Dr. Edward L. Bowles and Dr. David T. Griggs from Secretary of War Stimson's office, Louis Hagemeyer, a War Department photographer, whose job was to record the event, and of course Igor Sikorsky and others from the factory who had built the helicopters. At six o'clock the following morning the *James Parker* weighed anchor and got under way. All helicopter operating personnel were on deck prior to six A.M., and at that hour take-offs and landings began. Take-off and landing experience was desired while the ship was underway, yet in calm water.

As the ship proceeded farther and farther out in the ocean, the roll and pitch of the vessel increased and the air above her platform-deck became more turbulent, making the landings trickier. But pilot personnel experienced little difficulty in nego-

YR-4 and XR-4 on deck of James Parker.

Eddie Aldrin, Ben Chidlaw, Frank Gregory, and Erick Nelson aboard the James Parker.

tiating their landings and take-offs. It was clearly demonstrated that the landing deck was in the best possible location, at the stern of the ship. Some of the take-offs and landings that were made could never have been accomplished under similar wind conditions on the *Bunker Hill*. As it was, when the helicopters approached for a landing on the *James Parker*, if the approach wasn't just right the pilots would go backwards or to either side and come in again. There really wasn't much danger to it.

Once Lieutenant Hermes brought the XR-4 in for an approach and placed the main wheels on the deck while the craft's tail extended outward over the *Parker*'s side. Needless to say, we were very much relieved that he continued to fly it and took off from the deck, making another approach, this time coming in and sitting right on the bull's-eye.

There were actually three squares painted on the deck. One was forty feet by forty feet, another was thirty by thirty, and still a third was twenty by twenty. Inside the smallest square was an eight-foot-diameter white bull's-eye. Most of the landings were made on the bull's-eye.

It was evident in all the landings that there was very little preference between the float-type gear and the wheeled gear. Both had their advantageous features. The wheels were lighter and also afforded mobility while the helicopter was on the deck. On the other hand, the floats didn't slip or roll during landing procedure and this was their chief advantage. But YR-4 was awkward to handle on the deck; consequently we always landed it on the desired spot on the deck. It was believed that the ideal landing gear would be light shock-absorber struts with pads on the bottom so they would not slide about on the deck and a pair of attachable wheels which could be snapped on to make the helicopter easy to move about. This was recommended in case such operations were to be carried out on a large scale.

The second day out brought a real test. When we went out on deck in the early morning, fog was enveloping the ship and a fairly brisk wind was blowing. It was the kind of weather that would have made airplane pilots aboard a carrier desire to go back into the lounge for a day of poker, but it was good for our test operations. We wanted to try out the helicopter when it was rough and the waves were increasing by the minute. The wind over the deck reached a velocity of approximately forty miles per hour. The ship rolled about ten degrees and the deck surface moved about, much like a raft in rough water. Yet, despite these conditions, landings and take-offs were carried out with little trouble. This fact was most encouraging.

Rain came with the storm, however, and that curtailed operations. In order to protect the fabric on the blades of the helicopters' rotors, the two aircraft were landed and tied down to the deck with the special stilts we had devised at Sikorsky's plant. It must be remembered that the tip of a blade travels at approximately 300 miles per hour and the rain acts very much as a sand blast with respect to the fabric and eats the skin away on the leading edge. This could cause serious trouble in the control of a helicopter and is one of the problems yet to be solved. The development is most promising and has since progressed to a state that enables helicopters to fly in rain with a fair degree of protection to the covering.

A summary of the tests follows. Flight operations were conducted in the open sea more or less continuously on both the seventh and the eighth of July. During this, and the time at anchor, a total of 162 landings and take-offs were made, with a flying time of approximately twenty hours. Air work was divided about equally between the two helicopters, with both aircraft operating simultaneously for the greater part of the time. Weather varied from clear and unlimited to 200-foot ceilings, and one and a half mile's visibility with light fog and drizzle. Some rain was experienced on the morning of the seventh which was heavy enough to cause suspension of flight operations. The *James Parker* maneuvered to generate relative winds from all directions, and velocities of wind over the deck varied from zero to approximately forty miles per hour. The greatest rolling during operations was approximately ten degrees, with a fifteen-second period for a complete cycle of roll. While castored cradles were provided for the floats, deck spotting was done by landing the helicopter under its own power at the desired spot. No radio tests were made; although the YR-4 carried a transmitter and receiver, radio silence was maintained. The helicopters were flown with and without passengers. Their gross weight varied between 2250 and 2500 pounds. Operation and control at all times were entirely satisfactory despite the turbulence caused by the superstructure stack and masts of the ship.

About three o'clock in the afternoon of the second day out, the shoreline of Long Island loomed in the distance and Colonel Cooper in the XR-4 and Lieutenants Hermes and Peterson in the YR-4 took off from the deck and headed for the Sikorsky landing field, where both helicopters underwent a complete inspection. Theirs had been a rigid test and they had helped make aeronautical history.

20
The YR-4 Goes North

ON NOVEMBER 6, 1943, Lieutenant Colonel Les Cooper took delivery for the Army of a new YR-4B helicopter at the Sikorsky factory. After a series of test flights, he took off from the small fenced-in helicopter flying field behind the factory and a few minutes later landed at the Bridgeport airport beside a large C-46 Army transport plane. That was the beginning of a new adventure for the helicopter. The YR-4 was on her way to the land of the northern lights—Alaska.

The Army wanted information regarding the adaptability of the helicopter to extreme cold-weather operation. Consequently, this particular helicopter was on its way to Ladd Field, near Fairbanks, Alaska, where the AAF's cold-weather research base is located. The distance is approximately 4000 miles from Bridgeport, and, since helicopters are hardly at their best for long-haul operations, it was decided to test the feasibility of shipping one by cargo plane. Thus the experiment was twofold in its purpose —to try transporting helicopters by air and to run exhaustive tests with the machines in the cold Alaskan weather over the rough terrain of our isolated territory.

The C-46 is popularly known as the "Commando." It is the largest of any twin-engined transport in use by the AAF. Originally built by the Curtiss-Wright Corporation, the craft was snatched by the Army from its jig cradle. Ripped out were all the fancy trimmings of its interior, for which commercial air travelers will have to wait until the war's end to enjoy. She became an aerial mule and since has been plying the air routes of the world with the Air Transport Command. She tasted the blood of combat in Sicily and Italy and was used extensively to carry paratroopers, infantrymen, and supplies for the invasion forces. The ship is so large that she sits high enough off the ground for an averaged-sized man to walk beneath her wings without ducking. Special gangplanks are needed to load jeeps and other large equipment aboard. These she swallows up like the proverbial whale swallowed Jonah. It is easy to see why the C-46 was selected to carry the helicopter.

Before the YR-4B was built, the engineers of the Matériel Command charged with Army helicopter development had been thinking of transporting helicopters by air. Early in 1943, the helicopter was considered for an emergency mission to Greenland to rescue, from the treacherous ice floes of the white continent, several stranded AAF airmen who were forced down

there. To be useful in time, due to its limited cruising range, the helicopter would have to be transported by air to a near-by operational base. Thus, ten months before Les Cooper departed on the Alaskan mission, the Army was working on plans to transport by air its R-4 models. This rescue mission was never undertaken, however, since the rescue was effected by other means.

It was one thing to place on paper the measurements of a piece of cargo and apply these to the space available in the airplane. It was quite another problem actually to accomplish the job when the tolerances are close. Small models of the helicopter and the C-46 were built and men played with the toys. They figured out, using the models, how best the helicopter could be broken down, disassembled, and loaded into the big plane's cargo cabin. Consequently, when the Alaskan expedition was decided upon they knew how it was to be done.

Both AAF mechanics and servicemen from the Sikorsky plant were on hand at the airport when Les Cooper landed, and they began immediately to take the YR-4B apart. The ship, could it express its feelings, must have felt strange, for only a few days before the same men had worked equally as hard to put her together and get her ready for flight tests.

First the main rotor and tail rotor blades were removed. Then the ship was split into two sections. One consisted of the crew and engine compartments; the other was the long tail section which contained the main rotor transmission, fuel and oil tanks, and the tail rotor drive shaft. When this was done, the actual loading began. Next the undercarriage and tail wheel structure were stripped off the fuselage.

A special cradle was made for the individual rotor blades, and these were placed on the floor of the C-46 fuselage. It was soon evident that this arrangement was obstructive to crew egress and also offered too many chances for damage to the blades themselves. Therefore the blades, in their cradles, were slung to overhead structural members. Both the cabin and tail of the helicopter were secured to the floor and walls of the transport's cabin. The tail rotor assembly, rotor head, and spare parts were padded, boxed, and fastened down in the rear cargo section of the C-46. In this knock-down condition the YR-4B made the long air trip cross-country to Minneapolis and thence north over the lakes and swamps and crevasses of the Bush Flyer's domain to Ladd Field.

TESTS. . . . GENERAL BEHAVIOR OF SHIP SMOOTHER THAN AT ANY TIME PREVIOUS. . . . FLIGHTS INCLUDED BACKWARD AND FORWARD FLIGHT APPROXIMATED AT 12 TO 15 MILES PER HOUR. SIDEWAYS FLIGHTS MADE INDICATED ADEQUATE CONTROL.

Another wire from Sikorsky on September 13, 1943, indicated that progress was being made. It said: TOOK OFF TODAY WITH TEN PERSONS ON BOARD AND STILL SOME RESERVE POWER. USEFUL LOAD WAS 600 POUNDS ABOVE CONTRACT.

Morris had flown the ship on this test. There were two people in the cabin in normal seating arrangement and four others clung to each side of the aircraft, sitting on the landing-gear struts. The demonstration was to estimate the load-carrying capacities of the XR-5. The result was encouraging.

The new helicopter was demonstrated in flight to me by Les Morris on October 11, 1943. The event consisted of a vertical take-off to an altitude of about ten feet, hovering at that altitude for several minutes, and then rising vertically to an altitude of approximately 100 feet. The estimated rate of ascent to this altitude was approximately 800 feet a minute. The aircraft was then flown forward to speeds up to seventy-five m.p.h. These flights were smooth in all respects.

It was my pleasure to fly the aircraft after this initial demonstration. Morris kept his position in the rear seat; I was up front. We did the same maneuvers and then he turned the controls over to me so I could get the feel of the new helicopter.

In a report about this flight I wrote: "There was considerable difficulty in controlling the aircraft while hovering. This was believed due to the differences in the natural period of the aircraft from that of the YR-4 types. However, after a very few minutes of experimentation with the stick and pedals, the aircraft was brought under control. After approximately twenty minutes of flying from the observer's position I transferred to the pilot's position and continued to fly the craft for about a quarter of an hour. The ship was flown through all helicopter flight attitudes from backward flight to forward speed of approximately seventy-five m.p.h. and was excellently controlled through all maneuvers. The XR-5 has ample power and it is predicted will meet and in some cases surpass the guaranteed performance."

The rest of that report I hated to prepare. In itself it told the story of heartbreaks and disappointment: "On Tuesday, October 12, 1943, additional flights were scheduled but not made as the XR-5 was damaged while being flown by Jim Viner, one of the contractor's test pilots. There was a structural failure in the tail rotor. Just exactly what failed has not yet been determined. A complete investigation is now under way. The tail rotor and approximately the last four feet of the tail cone were broken completely and were only hanging to the aircraft by the control cables. This failure started when the XR-5 was approximately seventy feet in the air and the tail rotor and tail cone end were seen by ground observers to be hanging while the aircraft was still approximately thirty-five feet in the air. The aircraft was landed by the pilot, though there was no torque compensation. The fuselage naturally was turning in an opposite direction to that of the rotor, and upon reaching the ground, the left landing gear folded in the horizontal plane back against the fuselage, allowing the aircraft to roll on its side, thereby causing the main rotor to strike the ground. It is estimated that the damage is approximately twenty-five per cent. It is interesting to note that during this unfortunate incident, the pilot was capable of landing the aircraft without injury to himself or to the observer."

As a result of the crackup, from October 12 to November 25 we were without an XR-5 helicopter. Other models were in the process of fabrication and the next ship in line was rushed to completion. It was still called the XR-5 and was an identical aircraft. On Thanksgiving Day, 1943, Les Morris flew the craft for one minute, one inch above the ground. The control stick was extremely stiff laterally and it was difficult to actuate control of the ship, so the flights were discontinued. The second model of the XR-5 had flown.

Succeeding flights showed steady improvement. By January 26, 1944, the aircraft had been flown a total time of eight hours and fifteen minutes. The control difficulties were partially whipped and the craft was performing exceedingly well. It demonstrated good flight characteristics. The Army was certain it had a good "workhorse" in the XR-5. An acceptance inspection was made February 22, 1944. Meanwhile the model was put in production.

Soon there will be a number of R-5 helicopters, the production models, flying in the skies over U. S. towns and cities. Others are going to duty with the Navy and some are destined for Great Britain for co-ordination work with the Royal Navy, the RAF, and the ground forces. They may play a major part in any invasion. The helicopters that remain in this country will go to liaison and rescue squadrons for practicable work and utilization tests.

The XR-5 will get its chance to prove itself as a "lookout in the sky."

22
The Army-Navy
Helicopter

WITH THE ADVENT of the XR-4 and its successes, interest in the helicopter ballooned in aeronautical circles. A few in the Army were sold on this new type of aircraft. There was, we were certain, a great future for such an aircraft. Militarily, it was a new "secret weapon" for which we had been waiting a long time. The Navy saw in it a craft suitable for antisubmarine missions and an ideal scout aircraft. British experts in this country were anxious to get preparations under way in England for helicopter training. The aircraft that some people said was "impossible and impractical" was here and here to stay.

That was the general situation in May of 1942, before we had the XR-4 at Wright Field, a year before the first YR-4 had ever flown. But we knew then there was a new era ahead; an enthusiastic development program for the helicopter was being formulated. The task was threefold: to buy enough YR-4 helicopters so that we could expedite a test program and learn more about this unique performing aircraft; to build a larger ship that was to be the XR-5; to work out refinements in the YR-4 designs which would give that ship a more versatile utility. That refinement in its final analysis was a new aircraft. We called it the XR-6, a streamlined, high-powered, small helicopter.

Actually the XR-6 was born in the design stages of the YR-4 aircraft. We knew the YR-4's would have limited utility, but they would give us valuable information and we could get them quickest. These ships were too heavy for the horsepower installed. They couldn't carry enough and their performance was marginal. Installations such as bomb racks, radio equipment, and other military necessities made them even heavier and decreased performance even more. Some big changes were needed. It was decided to take one of the YR-4's and install a new and more powerful engine, streamline it, improve it. All considered, we had a new design to build, so much so that the idea of modifying a YR-4 was dropped. The idea of refinement of the type still persisted and as early as September 16, 1942, it was recommended that we spend an estimated half million dollars to buy four XR-6 aircraft, the ship to be a two-place, side-by-side helicopter of a new design, powered with a 225-h.p. Lycoming engine. The recommendation was not unfavorably considered.

XR-6 came near dying between conception and birth. While I was touring the country with the first British mission to visit the United States, a decision was reached at the Matériel Command to reject the whole idea. There was still some convincing to be done. The Navy helped save the day. In Washington with Commander Morton K. Fleming, Bureau of Aeronautics, we discussed the Navy's request for an order of four YR-4 helicopters. We agreed that the XR-6 would be a more desirable craft to do the job the Navy wanted done. It was this co-operative support—Army and Navy co-ordination in a home-front battle—that revived the experimental program and gave new life to the XR-6 helicopter.

It was more than a verbal support that the Navy contributed to the project. The Army was going to contract for five XR-6 aircraft, but the Navy transferred sufficient funds to foot fifty-three per cent of the bill. That meant three of the aircraft would go to the Navy, the remaining two for the Air Forces. Changes issued later brought the Army costs from forty-seven to fifty-seven per cent of the total expenditure. It was agreed, however, that the helicopters were to be built entirely to Army specifications. This was only logical, since the XR-6 design was the direct result of conferences between Matériel Command engineers and the Sikorsky experts. The contract was based on a one-dollar fixed fee plus cost. The cost was estimated at approximately $800,000.

There were the usual design and engineering conferences, but XR-6 grew progressively and by December of 1942 she was mocked up and ready for inspection. The first model XR-6 was rolled out of the plant about nine months later in September of 1943 for preliminary engine rev-up and general over-all function tests. These trials were made, however, minus the rotors because the usual vibration tests had not yet been applied to the aircraft. Vibration tests are known to be essential to all rotary-wing-aircraft experiments, as a result of the resonance and vibration experience that occurred with the early trials of the Autogiros. These tests are conducted by Matériel Command engineers using specially designed vibration-recording equipment. Thus it is possible to determine prior to initial flight any mechanical instability that might exist in the aircraft. It is a safety measure to insure flyability of the rotary-wing craft. In the case of the XR-6 it was discovered that the rotor had an unstable condition at a certain r.p.m. Tests showed that if the rotor were revved up quickly this instability was not considered hazardous, as this would allow passing through the critical rotor speed to higher speed before the vibrations could build up to severe magnitude. Otherwise the new helicopter was pronounced ready for flight tests. The mechanical instability was later removed by changing the natural frequency of certain parts of the aircraft.

Outwardly the XR-6 is the most streamlined helicopter ever built. It looks like a gourd with rotors and wheels. More accurately, perhaps, she simulates the XR-4 in configuration, but the squared edges are replaced with smooth-curved surfaces and by contrast she's like a modern sport coupé beside a Model T. We call her the "streamlined baby." She's all that and a helicopter too.

Into her construction and skin covering have gone some of the "magic materials" that have come into being, the products of necessity since the outbreak of the war. Like the XR-5 she is built in three sections, cabin, center section, and tail cone. Her engine and rotor shaft are supported by a welded-steel tubular structure cowled with a paper-base plastic. The cabin is built of molded plastic-impregnated glass-fiber cloth mounted on an aluminum alloy monocoque floor, which runs back underneath the center section much the same as the keel of a ship. The tail cone is built up of aluminum-alloy bulkheads and longérons covered with a tough magnesium skin.

The whole craft rests on a conventional landing gear; the two main wheels have cantilever struts. This means that all auxiliary supporting structure has been eliminated, cutting down resistance. There is a small tail wheel located mid-distance between nose and tail. In addition there is a small nose wheel which is used to protect the craft in the event of any tendency to nose over. It also improves forward taxiing capabilities.

Cabin interior has a side-by-side seating arrangement. Controls are identical to the YR-4. The nose, of one piece of molded plexiglass, affords excellent vision. Its optical properties are so perfectly formed that a mechanic visually inspecting a rudder pedal from the outside butted his nose against the clear glass front. A shelf directly behind the seats and about shoulder high holds a standard high-frequency radio communication set. There are also special pocketlike containers for maps and other flying paraphernalia.

The XR-6 is powered with an air-cooled Franklin six-cylinder, horizontally opposed 245-horsepower engine. Originally the ship was to have as its power plant a 225-horsepower Lycoming engine, but this engine was delayed in its development stages. The engine drives the rotor through shaft and gear transmission. It also drives the tail rotor by a long shaft and gears as on previous helicopters; this rotor shaft is inside the tail cone, a hinged portion of which permits inspection. The gasoline tank is located between the engine and the seat. Exhaust stacks and air intakes which cool the engine exhale and inhale through an opening in the side of the fuselage, but there are no protrusions to interfere with the ship's streamlining.

The rotor blades on the XR-6 are the same size as on the YR-4 ships. The blades are interchangeable with the YR-4 blades. The hub, however, is different. It is more compact and is mechanically improved. The prime virtue here is that it offers less drag.

The craft has a top speed in excess of 100 miles per hour. It can carry in its main tanks enough gasoline to remain aloft for more than five hours. Its normal gross weight is under 2600 pounds. It has sufficient ceiling to cross the Rockies with plenty of room to spare. She will climb to 5000 feet in less than seven minutes. There are provisions for carrying one litter in a capsule enclosure on each side of the fuselage. In lieu of these litters bomb racks can be installed.

This was the helicopter that made its first flight on October 15, 1943. Again Les Morris was at the controls, but the flight was anything but successful. It got off the ground and that was all. Morris had to exert considerable strength to hold onto the stick, which had a tendency to whip around in his hands. The ship was never more than a foot off the ground at any instant during the flight. There were three main faults with the XR-6: rough control stick, stiff rudder, and a heavy down load in the lift lever.

Forty days later the XR-6 had been in the air a total of only one hour and twenty-five minutes. Les Morris was still the only one to have flown her. Various changes in control adjustments were made, mechanical boosters were applied to the lift lever, and other minor corrections were made. There was always definite improvement, but troubles still existing had to be eliminated.

During a hovering flight, the clutch slipped under certain conditions. The transmission had a tendency to overheat—the same trouble we had with the XR-4. It heated up during hovering flight at the rate of approximately five degrees every thirty seconds. At speeds up to sixty or seventy miles per hour in forward flight, excessive vibration was still present. The XR-6, however, showed progress. We were sure that in this ship we had a real helicopter.

The author made his first flight in the craft with Les Morris on November 27, 1943. She was still rough, and it took both of us to fly her. But these were growing pains. The aircraft was sound as a thoroughbred colt and just as wild. What we had to do was to tame her. That same day six men were put on the ship, including two in the cabin. With the men aboard plus twenty-eight gallons of gas the craft hovered for several minutes, showing off her weight-lifting prowess.

Successive flights with the craft were made to check its various reactions to minor adjustments and improvements made after each flight. It was a long, tough job getting her in a satisfactory condition. The year 1944 was here before I actually flew the craft. There was considerable vibration and the rudder pedals were uncomfortable relative to the seat position, but other than these features the craft was extremely easy to fly. Most of the bugs were being eliminated. More work yet was required.

Snow flurries whirled about from out of nowhere and the temperature dropped below freezing. A couple of flights were made purposely to see if we couldn't determine reactions to icing conditions. There was no indication of ice building up on the blades, so flights were discontinued. But there is irony in the story. Since we've been flying helicopters, the specially trained small group of pilots are the only airmen who jump at a chance to fly when the weather has closed in and other aircraft are grounded. They have added a new term for the weatherman to ponder—"helicopter weather."

The XR-6 was showing signs by the end of the first month of 1944 of doing the things predicted of her. All who have flown her are most enthusiastic.

Her cabin is soundproofed; there is only a steady purring noise, and you can talk as though you were sitting side by side in a bus. She is very controllable and indeed a pleasure to fly. Proof of her flying characteristics and performance was brought out conclusively on March 2, 1944, when I flew the ship from the Washington National Airport to Patterson Field, Ohio, a distance of approximately 387 miles. The flight was made nonstop, with a reported headwind of from ten to thirty miles per hour, in four hours and fifty-five minutes. This flight made with a passenger, Ralph Alex, unofficially broke three world records. It was the longest nonstop flight in the history of the helicopter. The length of time in the air far surpassed the previous records, of-ficial or otherwise. The actual ground speed of the XR-6 was in excess of the world's record high speed.

There is an adventurous future ahead for her. Already in production, ships of this type soon will be in the skies over our countryside. More important, they will be out in the field, with the troops, doing an important job. Some will go to General Kenney and General MacArthur in the Southwest Pacific Theater. Others will be in England, in Africa, in Italy. The helicopter is at long last going to war, not only as an observation craft, but, side by side with the XR-5's also slated for delivery to active war zones, the XR-6 will perform many important missions.

Ground and air commanders will in all probability be transported from general headquarters to advanced base units fighting in the jungles of New Guinea or Burma. They will climb into this new streamlined helicopter and fly to the isolated Army groups, make their contacts, and return.

Out of the sky over some advanced Red Cross unit, serving the wounded on any battle front, an R-6 helicopter will drop to remove the more seriously injured in her specially developed litters. From the arctic to the jungles, the helicopter will be a new ship of mercy.

No longer are these predictions hearsay, no longer merely words and ideas. The XR-6 has made them realities. It is the helicopter for such tasks. Before many more months this helicopter you have read about will be doing all these things, a pioneer tactical development grown suddenly strong on the faith and sweat and courage of the men who believed in her.

23
Other Helicopters

THE NEWS SPEAKS for itself. The helicopter, though still in its infancy, is definitely growing. The Army Platt-LePage, Sikorsky, and other developments have pioneered the way. Now there are numerous new designs in progress. Two of these have already flown successfully; others have gotten off the ground with success comparable to the earlier attempts. Several still newer craft are in the test-flight stage. A big nationally famous bus line has filed petition to use helicopters for interurban service. One of the big airlines is planning a helicopter airport-to-downtown taxi business. Major schools and colleges like N. Y. U. and Princeton already have courses in helicopter design and theory. Other universities plan to follow suit. These are the trends.

In the small back-yard space of the Helicopter Corporation of America on Long Island one day in 1940, a new twin coaxial, superimposed, rotored helicopter with Boris Sergievsky, a Russian World War I ace, at its controls took off a few inches, staggered, shook, and landed. Its designer was Professor George de Bothezat, who died a few days before the flight was made. Ironically, the craft was about as successful as his first helicopter experiment for the Army in 1922.

The fuselage of the new de Bothezat helicopter is shaped like a fish and looks like one. The machine came into being after two years of experimental and construction work. The ship has three-bladed rotors, each blade resembling the wide, thin blade of a high-altitude propeller. A small Franklin engine is installed above the fuselage and between the upper and lower rotors. The rotors turn in opposite directions.

Control of the machine is accomplished with standard rudder and wheel controls of an airplane. The whole engine unit and the rotors are tilted in the desired direction of control. The gasoline tank is built in and around the power unit, with provision for free wheeling of the blades in the event of engine failure, to enable the pilot to land. The machine has a four-wheeled landing gear, two main wheels, nose wheel, and tail wheel. It is a single-place helicopter.

A more successful design is the "Bellicopter." Since the company came into existence, the Bell Aircraft Corporation of Buffalo, New York, has been famous for its revolutionary aircraft designs. It developed the experimental Airacuda, twin-engined, cannon-firing, pusher, multiplace, fighter plane; brought into being the cannon-packing, engine-in-the-center Bell Airacobra fighter, one of the best low-altitude planes of the war; and recently astounded the world with its twin-unit, jet-propelled fighter, the AAF's best-kept secret development. It has also built helicopters. They, too, are revolutionary—two-bladed rotors, open cockpit and closed cabin, light planes of the helicopter category.

In its general arrangement the Bell helicopter is similar to the Sikorsky type. The engine is a Franklin six-cylinder, horizontally opposed design developing approximately 150 horsepower, mounted directly beneath the main rotor, with the crankshaft turning in the vertical plane. Cockpit arrangement is directly in front of the engine, having a single seat with room for two persons, like the seating arrangement in an automobile. Behind the engine a tubular welded-steel outrigger, much like that on the VS-300, extends aft, with the torque-counteracting tail rotor, a twin-bladed propeller, mounted on the extreme end.

The main rotor is approximately thirty-four feet in diameter and has only two blades. Each blade is approximately ten inches in width. These blades are constructed of laminated wood. They are not independently articulated as are the blades of the XR-4 and the succeeding Army-Sikorsky types. They are, however, articulated as a complete unit, but relative to each other they are mounted rigidly like a variable-pitch propeller. Below the rotor and at right angles to the rotor blades is a rod of approximately one inch in diameter with streamlined counterweights on each end. This operates on the same principle as a flywheel and is connected with the control mechanism in such a manner as to operate as a stabilizing device.

Control of the Bell helicopter is actuated by rocking the two blades of the rotor about the hub, which in effect is the same as cyclic pitch change. It has the same effect on the aircraft.

The first of the craft, built in the latter part of 1942 and early 1943, was flown in spring of 1943 in its skeletonized-structure form. It had only a nose cowling and the rest was all exposed welded-steel tubing. Its landing gear consisted of four dural tubes of approximately three inches in diameter and twelve feet long. The ends of these tubes were mounted on the fuselage

Canvas litter capsule on side of YR-4.

XR-6 with one litter on each side.

Higgins helicopter.

PART II

And Even More

25

A Dramatic
Quarter Century

Shortly before ten o'clock the night of November 4, 1958, a worker's kerosene lamp exploded in the nearly completed main terminal building of Brussels' new twenty-four-million-dollar airport. The flash of fire set off a chain of events climaxed about forty minutes later by one of the most dramatic helicopter rescues on record.

The rescued: Marcel Courtoy, control-tower operator, and Guillaume Michaux, signal man. The rescuers: Gerard Tremarie, chief helicopter pilot for Sabena, Belgium's airline; Armand Adam, Sabena's maintenance manager for helicopters, and Charles Gillet, an inspector. Their performance was one of skill and calmness in an emergency where time permitted only split-second decisions and where a wrong move would have spelled disaster for all five men.

In the new control tower, almost 155 feet above ground level, Courtoy and Michaux first noticed smoke about 9:45 P.M. Courtoy phoned the airport fire department. The towermen probably could have made their way down and out of the building at that time, but duty dictated that they stay at their posts to make emergency phone calls and clear all aircraft from the building area. Then, only minutes later, it was too late to escape.

Courtoy's watch showed 9:56 when the smoke became so dense that it was impossible to stay any longer in the tower. "We're leaving now," he shouted into his microphone. Then he and Michaux dashed through a rear door and leaped to the roof about eight feet below. The roof, about seventy feet long and forty-five feet wide, jutted out at a right angle to the main terminal building, forming, in effect, the base of the T that is the building's shape.

Flames feeding on the wood scaffolding of the partly finished building roared up an elevator shaft adjacent to the tower. Smoke poured from windows below, forcing the towermen to run quickly from spot to spot to find clear air. They went to the rear of the building and looked down the sheer face of the structure to a crowd gathering 145 feet below. Firemen raised a ladder but it was six feet short. Courtoy, sensing that only one avenue remained to escape from the choking smoke, shouted: "Send a helicopter!"

The action shifted to the home of Armand Adam, a mile and a half away. A phone call from the airport informed Adam that there was a fire at the terminal. He jumped into his car, raced to the Sabena hangar, and rounded up his helicopter maintenance crew of twenty men. Fixed-wing crews on duty raised the Sabena total to about 150 men; all headed for the terminal building to lend what help they could.

Adam, meanwhile, remained at the Sabena hangar to alert his night shift, which was due in at 10:15 o'clock. It was then that he received word that men were trapped in the control tower and that the firemen could not reach them. Could he do something?

"We pulled aircraft OO-SHG, the oldest S-58 we had, from the hangar," Adam recalled. "We removed the two cabin doors, attached a heavy rope onto the cabin seats, and tied a shoulder harness to the rope. This is a safety harness used by our photographer during photo flights. The idea was to hover over the tower and pick up the men with the harness."

Adam next telephoned Tremarie, whose apartment is about six miles from the airport, and told him of the trapped men. "Gerry asked no explanations," Adam recalled. "He just ran for his car." Adam then asked for a volunteer to help him pull in the trapped men and chose the first man to step forward, the youthful Gillet. The helicopter's engine was started, the rotor blades began to turn, and all was ready for the pilot's arrival.

"It was amazing what Armand had done in the ten minutes it took me to drive to the airport," Tremarie recalled. "He had pulled out the ship, completed preflight inspection, warmed up the engine, removed the doors, and installed the rope and harness. Thirty seconds after I stepped from my car, we were in the air."

Tremarie flew the helicopter in a slow circle over the

Frank Gregory and Igor Sikorsky autograph copies of
Anything A Horse Can Do.

flaming building, looking for the men on the roof, determining wind direction and the best way to effect the rescue. The hot, turbulent air made it difficult to stabilize the aircraft in a hover, so he quickly abandoned the harness-pickup idea and decided to land on the smoke-shrouded roof. As the first circle was completed, the helicopter crew spotted the two men huddled at one corner of the roof, caught in a glare of spotlights from the ground and by the copter's own landing light. It was now obvious that without help soon they would suffocate. Tremarie circled again, letting down at a steep angle that would enable him to auto-rotate into a parking area below in case of engine failure.

Tremarie brought the helicopter over the edge of the building, set it down gingerly, and maintained enough lift on his blades to keep about twenty percent of the aircraft's weight off the roof. Radio antennae and supporting wires loomed perilously close to his tail rotor, cutting the available landing space down to about a forty-five-foot square.

As the helicopter landed, the rotor downwash cleared a small area within the cloud of billowing smoke. The downwash also fed fresh air to the carburetor.

When the aircraft touched down, Courtoy and Michaux dashed to the left side of the copter and attempted to remove an emergency door. Adam and Gillet then leaped to the roof, ran around in front of the aircraft, and led the towermen to the right side of the copter and through the main cabin door. Adam ran back toward the tower to make sure that there was nobody else on the roof. He reentered the copter and advised Tremarie over the intercom that there was nobody else trapped. Tremarie made a smooth takeoff and landed the S-58 in front of the Sabena hangar. The time: 10:35 P.M., only fifteen minutes after Adam had first been told that there were men trapped in the control tower.

Tremarie, a much-decorated veteran of many helicopter mercy missions, including a number during the Holland floods of 1952, took a modest view of his exploit. An aftermath of the rescue left the most lasting impression on him.

"Courtoy and his wife came to my office the day after the fire," he said, "not to thank me, but to bring me something appreciated much more—a letter from their eight-year-old daughter, Suzanne."

The letter read: "How happy I am, sir, because you have brought back my dad before he burned. Thank you very much. I send you my best kiss from me, and kisses from my younger sisters, Colette and Monique, and my brother, Marcel, who cannot yet write."

This spectacular rescue, which would have been impossible with any other vehicle but the helicopter, is only one isolated example, merely a microcosm, of the helicopter's achievements of the past quarter century. In countless ways, spanning man's endeavors and touching upon an almost limitless list of his activities, the helicopter has more than fulfilled its promise as outlined in the earlier chapters of this book. It has grown bigger, faster, and more reliable than most of us early birds had predicted. Fitted with lightweight yet powerful turbine engines, it lifts greater payloads to higher altitudes than we had foreseen. And its versatility, as shown in day-to-day operation from tropics to Arctic, from oceans to mountaintops, has surpassed our fondest expectations. Indeed the more accurate phrase today would be "Anything a horse can do—and then some!"

Consider, for example, a few scenes that became commonplace as the years unfolded:

A small helicopter whirls low over a field in Colombia, South America, spraying the banana plants below. A larger helicopter totes a giant transmission tower over the hills of West Virginia. A third copter flies building materials to a craggy radar site in Greenland. A fourth speeds beneath low gray clouds to land a work crew on an oil rig in the Gulf of Mexico. A fifth sets a geologist down in the frozen silence of an Alaskan mountainside. A sixth snatches a downed American fighter pilot from an enemy-infested jungle in Southeast Asia. A seventh saves passengers and crew from a watery death as a ferry succumbs to mountainous waves in the Skagerrak Strait off Denmark. An eighth, a huge flying crane, precision places over two million pounds of heating and ventilating equipment on the roof of a new auto assembly plant near Pittsburgh, a job requiring three months by conventional methods. A ninth snatches scores from raging waters during the Connecticut flood in 1955. A tenth picks up the President of the United States on the White House lawn and speeds him (in air conditioned comfort) over the traffic jams below to his jet waiting at Andrews Air Force Base. The list could be continued indefinitely, but space prohibits it. In recent years the helicopter has come of age in three major areas, military, commercial, and, more recently, industrial.

Military

Helicopters have long since proved their usefulness for military operations and today are virtually indispensable to a modern fighting force. In World War II the R-4 served for liaison and behind-the-lines rescue missions in Burma, becoming known as "the only helicopter that went to war." In Korea, larger helicopters evacuated the wounded, flew reconnaisance flights over and around the rugged mountains, and sped troops and supplies to peaks,

The helicopter helps build 310-foot tower.

Delivery of heating unit for installation.

A landing field of canvas and snow.

President Richard M. Nixon prepares to board.

ridges, and other strategic spots. Before Korea, eighty to ninety percent of soldiers who suffered head or stomach wounds died. In Korea, quick transfer by helicopter from the battlefield to rear-area hospitals reduced this to ten percent. In Vietnam, the use of far larger numbers of modern turbine-powered helicopters as flying ambulances reduced the rate even more. For the badly wounded man the difference between a short helicopter flight and a bumpy jeep or truck ride of many hours was often the difference between life and death.

Vertical lift aircraft brought new mobility to the battlefield, making the U.S. Army the world's largest user of helicopters. Today's Army consists of small, fast-moving units scattered ten, twenty-five, or even fifty miles apart. The gaps between the units bring problems—bridgeless rivers, roadless swamps, or, as in Southeast Asia, jungles and enemy ambush. Supplying these scattered forces by surface vehicles is slow, risky, and often impossible. So the Army switched from wheels to wings, chiefly the rotary wings of helicopters ranging in size from nimble Hueys and OH-6As to big Chinooks and flying cranes.

Helicopter theories and predictions became facts in Vietnam, scene of the world's first helicopter war. Large numbers of airborne troops were landed with pinpoint accuracy and ready for combat deep within enemy territory. Huey transports, carrying from seven to thirteen troops each, flew high to avoid ground fire. At the landing zones, other Hueys dived down to strike the enemy with rocket and machine-gun fire after which the transports landed and the troops leaped out to take up battle positions. Then the transports took off, still protected by the armed copters, which also supported the troops on the ground. During this double-barreled blow at the enemy, ambulance helicopters sped the critically wounded out of the area. When the ground operation was completed the transports returned to fly the troops back to their home bases, high above the jungle trails and enemy ambush. Throughout the action the helicopters provided both transportation and protection.

Larger helicopters brought further strength to the Army's airborne attacks. Chinooks carried thirty-three troops each, while spindly-legged flying cranes, or Skycranes, carried bulky loads on external hoists. The Skycranes flew bulldozers to construction sites, artillery batteries to mountaintops, cargoes from ships to inland points, and retrieved downed aircraft, often from deep within enemy territory. The retrieval operations saved millions of dollars in damaged aircraft, many of which were repaired to fly again. Skycranes also carried detachable pods or vans, outfitted as mobile hospitals, command posts, and repair shops.

For the U.S. Marines the helicopter changed the face of amphibious warfare. From the American Revolution through the Korean conflict the Marines carried out more than two-hundred-eighty sea-to-land operations. However, with the arrival of the nuclear age it became clear that launching landing craft from closely packed ships offshore would henceforth prove a dangerous maneuver; such an amphibious force would be a sitting duck for one nuclear bomb. In 1946 the Marines turned to the helicopter, and developed a new tactic called "vertical envelopment." The tactic proved sound; with helicopters an amphibious force could be widely dispersed over the sea with far less vulnerability to air attack.

In 1958 large-scale maneuvers along the coast of North Carolina showed how the Marines' concept of assault landing had changed in only a few years. Waves of helicopters landed in clearings in the pine woods, pouring out infantrymen and tons of supplies. The Marines scattered into the woods. Only minutes before they and their equipment had been aboard aircraft carriers at sea. Now, hav-

A departure from offshore drilling rig.

On a drilling rig off shore.

Marines land from Boeing Vertol Ch-46.

Navy CH-46 lowers supplies to vessel at sea.

ing leapfrogged over the beaches, they were fifteen miles inland with their units intact and ready for action. Gone were the days of slugging it out across heavily fortified beaches as in World War II. One grizzled veteran summed it up when he said, "A landing without wet feet. What will the Marines come up with next?"

The Marines brought vertical envelopment to Vietnam, using at first the Sikorsky CH-34 and later the larger Boeing-Vertol CH-46 (seventeen to twenty-five troops each) and the still larger Sikorsky CH-53A (thirty-eight troops). The latter, which weighs almost eighteen tons fully loaded, carries the thirty-eight troops, or a four-ton payload, a distance of 115 miles at a speed of 172 miles an hour, then returns to base with a two-ton load without refueling. By using a winch system, one man can load or unload more than a ton of cargo a minute on an inclined ramp leading to a big rear door in the aircraft. The copter can be quickly changed from a troop to a cargo transport by folding the seats against the cabin walls. The cabin can also be quickly transformed into an ambulance with stretchers for twenty-four patients.

Antisubmarine warfare (ASW) is more important today than ever before in our history. Hidden beneath the waves, nuclear-powered submarines can launch nuclear destruction against our cities and industries. The U.S. Navy stands as the first line of defense against that threat, and the sonar-dipping helicopter has become one of its chief weapons. The Navy first experimented with the helicopter-sonar combination in 1945. Since then both sonar and helicopters have been much improved. Today's ASW helicopter, the Sikorsky SH-3D Sea King, cruises at 150 miles an hour and can fly four-hour missions. At night, in instrument flight weather, the helicopter's sonar dips are fully automatic. The pilot pushes a button and his automatic flight control system takes over, carrying him through a "hands-off" transition in speed and altitude and into an automatic hover forty feet above the water.

"The helicopter," said an ASW admiral several years ago, "used to be a fragile, fair weather, daylight vehicle. But now, in its second generation, it is an all-weather aircraft, asking no special treatment from anyone. Today we can use helicopters under conditions that would stop all other aviation—and we've done it."

Teamwork is the key word for the ASW effort. Navy ASW helicopters are part of large task forces each headed by an ASW aircraft carrier. Aboard each carrier are fixed-wing aircraft and helicopters, while destroyers and submarines ply the waters nearby. Far away, but also part of the team, are long-range, land-based airplanes carrying electromagnetic devices for detecting metal beneath the sea. The planes, with their greater speed and range, may be the first to locate a lurking sub. The helicopters

then rush to the scene to pinpoint the sub's exact position, to track it, and finally attack it with homing torpedoes. Other craft, if they are close enough, may join the attack.

In today's Navy the task of supplying and resupplying vessels at sea is carried out by a far-flung cargo transport system. Material moves in an endless flow from dockside warehouses to supply ships, which rendezvous with the fleet for final delivery. For many years the supply ships pulled alongside the destroyers, carriers, or other vessels while the cargoes were transferred by lines between the vessels, a difficult, time-consuming method, especially in stormy weather. Today, helicopters provide the final link, serving as flying trucks in what the Navy calls "vertical replenishment," lowering the supplies to the decks in cargo nets. The helicopters operate from the supply ships, which have landing platforms, hangars, and repair shops. The new method brings greater safety as well as speed, since the ship being supplied does not have to slow down or leave the security of its position with the fleet but can be supplied while steaming at full speed.

The Navy has found still other jobs for helicopters. Minesweeping is one. The conventional minesweeper operates at great risk, for it can be blown up by the very mines it is trying to cut adrift.

Search and rescue, as seen in the saving of pilots downed at sea by accident or enemy action, or in the recovery of astronauts after splashdown, are other helicopter missions handled by the Navy. Upon completion of all U.S. space flights, from the Mercury through the Gemini and Apollo programs, helicopters flying from the decks of aircraft carriers have served as the primary means of recovery. In almost every case the copters, airborne well before the space capsules reentered the earth's atmosphere, were the first to reach the spacecraft after splashdown. These many and varied uses of helicopters at sea recall vividly to mind the proof, first provided in 1943 aboard the *Bunker Hill* in Long Island Sound, that the helicopter, needing no large landing space, is especially suited to shipboard operation.

The helicopter, a vehicle in which appearance has always ranked second to function, has even made its way in the sleek jet world of the Air Force. Today's big missile bases encompass separate installations as far as one hundred fifty miles apart. SAC (Strategic Air Command) helicopters link these units, carrying men and equipment. Air Force copters supply remote radar stations, recover equipment parachuted into the ocean from space flights, and locate and pick up target aircraft, or drones. In 1963 a twin-turbine Air Force/Sikorsky CH-3C became the first helicopter ever to cross the Greenland icecap, cruising at thirteen-thousand feet to clear the icy peaks below. The crossing came during the copter's nine-and-a-

Sikorsky CH-53A supplies drop zone in Vietnam.

half day trip from Otis AFB, Cape Cod, Massachusetts, to the Paris Air Show. Forced to detour north by bad weather, the aircraft, named the *Otis Falcon*, covered 4,524 miles, the longest helicopter mission on record. Earlier, in 1952, two Air Force/Sikorsky H-19s, single-engined craft, became the first helicopters to fly across the Atlantic. Their route from Westover Field, Massachusetts, to Wiesbaden, Germany, was by way of Maine, Labrador, Greenland, Iceland, and the British Isles. The four-thousand-mile trip took twenty days and almost fifty-two flight hours.

Helicopters are performing an ever-increasing proportion of the worldwide work of the Air Force's Aerospace Rescue and Recovery Service (ARRS). This service, with personnel of over four thousand, has more than one hundred units in the United States and some twenty other countries and territories. Searching for missing airplanes, often in the wilderness, and directing evacuation of areas threatened by hurricanes are among its routine tasks. More demanding is the service's wartime duty of recovering combat air crews downed in enemy territory. Almost every recovery mission brings its moment of truth when the helicopter must come to a low hover to effect a pick-up by hoist. Holding such a hover while enemy fire rips through the helicopter takes more than usual courage. In Vietnam, ARRS crews first used little single-engined Kaman HH-43B Huskies, then, as recovery flights became longer, the larger twin-turbine-powered Sikorsky HH-3E "Jolly Green Giants," and finally the even larger, faster "Super Jolly Greens," Sikorsky HH-53Bs. During the war in Vietnam (until early in 1970) ARRS crews had saved some more than one thousand persons, many of them from certain capture or death. The rescue copters proved big morale builders among the crews of the jet fighters. "It's comforting to know," said one pilot, "that you'll get another chance."

The Jolly Green crews formed a close-knit group, proud of the ARRS motto "That Others May Live." In April 1969, eighty-five men met at Eglin AFB, Florida, to form the Jolly Green Pilots Association. Lieut. Col. Baylor Haynes, second in command of the ARRS Training Center at Eglin, said the association would hold annual meetings "to perpetuate the Jolly Green name and to enjoy the fellowship of an effort that we will forever remember with pride and satisfaction." Up until that time the Jolly Greens alone had made more than eight-hundred combat rescues in Vietnam. The achievement was not without its price: eighty-five heads were bowed as Col. Haynes read the names of seventeen Jolly Green pilots and crewmen killed, missing, or captured in Vietnam.

Present at the first reunion was George Martin, a retired captain, who on July 27, 1965, flew to within thirty-five miles of Hanoi to make the first Jolly Green rescue. Also on hand was Captain Gerald Young, holder of the Congressional Medal of Honor for an HH-3E rescue mission in 1967. Igor Sikorsky sent a taped message, describing the group's accomplishments as "one of the most glorious pages in the story of human flight," adding, "I am happy and privileged to express to you my deepest and most sincere friendship, respect, and admiration."

The helicopter's demonstrations of its growing reliability and all-around performance in recent years are so many and varied as to defy listing. No more convincing demonstration has occurred, perhaps, than the nonstop flight of two Air Force/Sikorsky HH-3Es from New York to Paris in 1967. The two copters, Jolly Green Giants, each carrying a crew of five, took off from the Naval Air Station, Brooklyn, New York, at 1:05 A.M., May 31. One, commanded by Major Herbert Zehnder, landed at Le Bourget Field at 12:51 P.M., June 1 (helicopter day at the Paris Air Show) and the other, commanded by Major Donald Maurras, touched down a few minutes later. Each helicopter had been refueled nine times in the air from Lockheed C-130 Hercules aircraft despite rain, snow, sleet, and ice. The HH-3Es were standard aircraft fresh from the production line and assigned to the 48th Aerospace Rescue and Recovery Squadron, Eglin AFB, Florida. They flew a route that followed Lindbergh's during the early stages, but then swung northward to pass close to Greenland and Iceland, making landfall in northern Scotland. They covered 4,270 miles compared with Lindbergh's 3,610.

Varying winds held the helicopters' ground speed to as low as 115 miles-per-hour at times, and at other times boosted it to as high as 170 miles-per-hour. The head-

Twin-jet Sikorsky for submarine detection.

Skycrane transports 155 millimeter field artillery piece.

Sikorsky S-58, owned by Okanagan Group, taking soundings on St. Lawrence Seaway.

telephone wires. The copter flew about five feet above the wires and the ice came cascading down. When thousands of hungry starlings settled on the vineyards in Germany's Neckar River Valley, helicopters were called to frighten them away—and the year's valuable grape crop was saved.

Ranch owners in the West and Southwest find that a single helicopter does the work of fifteen to twenty cowboys in herding cattle, patroling fences, and riding the range. In Utah, helicopters rounded up a herd of buffalo so that they could be vaccinated by government veternarians. Laying pipeline, supplying lighthouses and remote radar stations, carrying prospectors into unexplored territory and doctors into remote villages are only a few of the endless jobs done by civilian helicopters.

Logging with helicopters was first formally proposed at the 1947 Redwood Logging Conference and it has since been the subject of many theoretical studies. The introduction of the Crane concept and the evolution of production machines formed the basis of several current services that are really paying off. The early sling-loaded slurry buckets that were originally used to haul concrete have been replaced by light-weight, variable-capacity plastic buckets that carry fire retardants directly to critical targets.

These same machines and flight techniques have recently been employed to bring previously unrecoverable prime mature timber from inaccessible areas to nearby roadheads. The resultant minimized damage to the logging sites and residual stands of young timber combined with significant savings from inflated road, bridge, and other construction costs have made such an operation economically feasible for the first time.

A stripped-down version of the twin-turbine S61 was obtained along with expert operators from Wes Lamottas' Construction Helicopters of Portland, Oregon. Their services were contracted by Jack Erickson, who has a mill in Marysville, California, to log some inaccessible government timber in the Plumas National Forest. To date they have logged over four million board feet and have enough of a backlog to keep them busy until next fire season. A good day's productive work consists of up to two hundred trips of one- to two-minute duration. Each trip carries close to eight thousand pounds of logs suspended on a one hundred-foot cable. This unique type of operation has added a new dimensional challenge to reduce flight times in absolute terms of seconds instead of the traditional minutes and hours.

Executive helicopters, designed to provide portal-to-portal transportation for businessmen, have made their appearance. They fly from the front door (or the roof) of a plant or office building directly to an airport or other destination, saving hours of driving time. The world's busiest executive, the President of the United States, takes off from the White House lawn in a helicopter powered by two turbine engines and equipped with an air-conditioned cabin, desk, and telephone. Within minutes he lands at Andrews Air Force Base, ready to board the Presidential jet for a flight of hundreds or thousands of miles. At the end of his trip a helicopter speeds him over the traffic to his destination—swiftly and safely.

In New York, helicopters flying on regular schedules speed passengers between Kennedy, LaGuardia, and Newark airports. From Los Angeles International Airport, helicopter routes fan out north, east, and south to bring air service right to the doorsteps of communities twenty-five, fifty, and even seventy-five miles from the airport. In the San Francisco area, helicopters also serve as suburban connectors, linking San Francisco Airport with cities to the north and east across San Francisco Bay, and with Palo Alto, San Jose, and other communities to the south.

Helicopters also serve as airliners far from the multilane freeways of the big cities. They carry passengers hundreds of miles along the rugged west coast of Greenland, linking isolated villages with a big jetport at Sondrestrom from which flights go east to Copenhagen, and west to Los Angeles. Flying boats, which once provided this service, cannot operate in the long northern winter because of ice floes, and to carve airports from mountainsides would have been difficult and expensive. So the helicopters, needing only small, inexpensive helistops on which to land, again proved a natural answer.

The scheduled lines fly big twin-engined helicopters carrying up to twenty eight passengers at speeds of 140 miles an hour. Electronic devices give them such excel-

Sikorsky S-55 operated by Okanagan Helicopter LTD, on Alcan project in British Columbia.

*Sikorsky S-55, owned by Okanagan Group, working for
Dominion Department of Fisheries in Newfoundland.*

The Skycrane begins to lift the log.

The Skycrane in logging operations.

Skycrane shows its ability in logging.

Errands of mercy at sea.

On patrol.

Working with victim of storm and flood.

saving 138 persons, fifty-eight of them at night.

The helicopter's life-saving record in floods, hurricanes, and typhoons is worldwide. In Japan, in Germany, in the Netherlands, thousands of lives have been saved by copter crews who braved freezing temperatures, swirling waters, and winds up to eighty miles an hour. At times they broke through roofs with their landing wheels to allow trapped families to climb out through the holes and into the copters, and crewmen jumped onto slippery, sloping roofs to chop holes and free families trapped in attics.

In recent years hospitals have built small heliports on their grounds. A recent count showed 1,812 hospital heliports in all fifty states and Washington, D.C. The cost averages from one thousand dollars to three thousand dollars per heliport, but the minutes saved in flying the sick and injured directly to hospital doors has often been proved. The Coast Guard inspired construction of several hospital heliports in Florida and California, and its copters regularly rush patients to the sites.

Years after his Air Commando days in Burma, Colonel Phil Cochran summed up helicopter rescues simply during a chance meeting with Igor Sikorsky. "There are many guys alive today because you fulfilled your dreams," he said.

The helicopter quickly won its wings with the Coast Guard. Its ability to fly low and slow if necessary made it a natural for search missions, while hovering proved ideal for rescues. The need for speedy rescues has grown in recent years with the mushrooming popularity of pleasure boating. Previously, the Coast Guard's traditional job was taking surviving seamen off wrecked vessels. Today's Coast Guardsmen spend more time rushing aid to small cruisers or amateur fishermen in distress.

There is no end to the variety of search and rescue missions flown by Coast Guard helicopters: a motorboat out of fuel, a hunter lost in a swamp, a flaming collision of two oil tankers, a deckhand injured at sea, a man overboard, a swimmer caught in the undertow, a youngster trapped on a cliff, a sinking yacht, even a child bitten by a rattlesnake. Once a Coast Guard copter used the downwash of its rotor blades to blow a demasted sailboat away from the rocky shores of the Pacific near San Francisco so that a fishing craft could take her in tow.

Hurricane Betsy, in September 1965, led to the greatest airlift ever carried out by Coast Guard helicopters. In three days the copters, using rescue baskets at the ends of their hoists, carried 1,192 persons to safety from New Orleans and small towns to the south of the city. Helicopters whirled everywhere in the devastated area, playing vital roles as spotters, communications stations, and rescue vehicles.

The Coast Guard now uses amphibious helicopters that go right down onto the water to save victims, many of them too weak to grasp a line lowered from a hovering helicopter. The amphibious copter has a flying boat hull. When it alights on the water a crewman extends a rescue platform that folds out from the fuselage at water level. The survivor climbs or is pulled onto the platform, and within seconds finds himself safe inside the cabin. The copter's landing speed is zero. In rough seas the pilot can vary the lift of his rotor blades, keeping most of the weight of the craft on the blades while the hull rides lightly on the waves.

In its first rescue mission the combination of amphibian and rescue platform saved the life of a sailor. The copter, flown by Coast Guard Captain John M. Waters, Jr., was searching for two men missing from a wrecked fishing vessel off Point Judith, Rhode Island. The date was March 22, 1963, a bitterly cold day. Suddenly, Waters overheard a call from a Navy radar ship that a crewman had been washed overboard near Newport Harbor. He and his co pilot sped to the scene, spotted the radar ship, and quickly began searching astern. They found the man, alighted on the water, and hauled him into the cabin. He was blue with cold and could never have been saved by the hover-and-hoist method.

The Coast Guard continues to improve its helicopter fleet. New twin-turbine amphibians, almost twice as large as the original flying lifeboats, can fly three hundred miles out to sea to make rescues.

Future

One morning recently a traveler left Fairfield, Connecticut, at 6:30 o'clock to catch an 8:00 A.M. shuttle jet flight from LaGuardia Field to Washington National Airport where the scheduled arrival time was 9:00 A.M. Air traffic control problems delayed the departure from LaGuardia until 9:16, and there was further delay over Washington. The jet finally landed at 10:20 and the traveler reached his destination in downtown Washington at 10:47, some thirty minutes late for a scheduled meeting. His trip had taken more than four hours, twenty-five percent of which was scheduled air travel and less than fifteen percent actual point-to-point flight time.

The traveler's experience, by no means uncommon, points to one area in which the helicopter may well prove vital in the future—city center to city center airline operation over distances from fifty to two hundred miles. It points, also, to the need for a total transportation system geared to the total need of the traveler to move from his home or office to his final destination.

The "systems" approach, which has been successfully

Milk for villagers near Maknessi, Tunisia.

pioneered by the military services in applying aircraft to military missions, will have to be applied to the civilian transportation mission. Past practice has been to build more and larger airports and to improve road access to and from the airports. But this practice has become less and less successful with the skyrocketing growth of air travel. The resulting congestion both in the air and on the ground in the vicinity of the air terminals has already brought a marked slow-down in the rate of growth of air travel at major terminals.

In a conference room overlooking San Francisco International Airport, a group of city officials and helicopter airline executives spent two hours recently discussing the air terminal's future expansion. The talks were focused almost entirely on the growing problem of moving passengers to and from the airport, downtown, and the suburbs. One conclusion: at least six and maybe eight helicopter landing sites, all at ground level, will be needed at the airport in addition to the single rooftop site initially planned.

Twenty-five hundred miles east, at about the same time, at the plant of Sikorsky Aircraft in Stratford, Connecticut, helicopter designers and builders sat through two lengthy briefings in a week, absorbing from a battery of statisticians the high points of two separate, year-long studies of possible remedies for the nation's chaotic and largely ineffectual short-haul transportation. The studies outlined in detail how vertical-lift aircraft can help solve the problem.

In Washington, D.C., a few weeks earlier, the Civil Aeronautics Board issued an order to sixteen airlines to study the feasibility of "metropolitan area to metropolitan area air service," with the chief emphasis on vertical-lift aircraft, along the Northeast Corridor from Boston to Washington. The study was aimed at determining whether public convenience and necessity require the use of vertical takeoff and landing (VTOL) aircraft or short takeoff and landing (STOL) aircraft to link selected cities along the corridor. The ultimate aim, of course, was to cut the businessman's travel time by flying him directly from city center to city center, thus enabling him to bypass both air and ground congestion at the big air terminals.

These and similar activities throughout the country gave evidence of a growing public concern that increasingly congested surface transportation is wiping out much of the time savings brought to air travelers by the jet age.

Fifty percent of the commercial aircraft arrivals and departures from airports in the New York area are for aircraft involved in trips of three hundred miles or less. These trips alone involve more than thirty percent of all the domestic air passengers. Those who are studying the problem of airport congestion are increasingly asking the question, "Must these passengers go to the airport?" Increasingly, the answer is, "No." Everyone, the long-haul and the short-haul passenger, will benefit if the short flights are removed from the big air terminals. How will they be removed? One answer is the use of vertical-lift aircraft able to take off from relatively small city vertiports and land on similar vertiports in another city.

Bell AH-16 Hueycobras on check flight.

Navy Sikorsky SH-3D hoists astronaut Neil Armstrong after splashdown in the Pacific, July 24, 1969.

Coast Guard to the rescue.

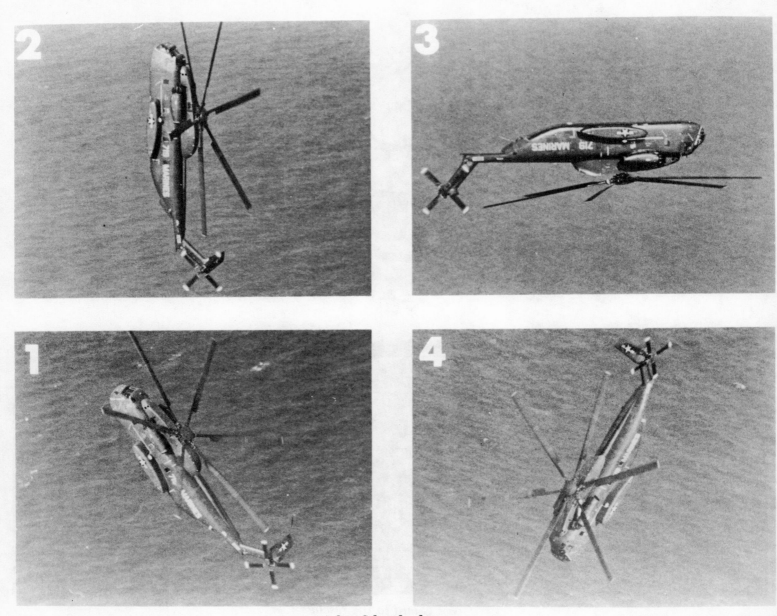

A big Sikorsky loops.

A big Sikorsky rolls.

Individual Index

Achgelis, 51, 60
Adam, Armand, 163 164
Aldrin, E. E., 125, 127
Alex, Ralph, 87, 88, 101, 144, 179
Archimedes, 19
Armstrong, Neil, 206
Arnold, Henry H., 66, 101
Ashenfelter L. C., 26

Bailey, F. J., Jr., 76, 84
Bane, Thurman H., 24, 25, 26, 28, 29
Baumhauer, 33
Beasley, R. W., 66
Beaty, Ed, 87
Beighle, Jackson, 199
Bell, Laurence, 145, 149, 151, 152, 176, 178, 180, 183, 194, 198, 205, 213, 217
Bennett, James Gordon, 21
Benson, J. W., 49
Berliner, Emile, 21, 32, 33, 42, 75
Berliner, Henry, 32, 43
Bienvenu, 19
Biggerstaff, John F., 47
Bleeker, Maitland B., 33, 40
Bogert, Howard Z., 75, 76, 91, 92, 138, 140
Boles, John Keith, 57
Bossi, Enea, 150
Botting, W. J., 26
Bowles, Edward L., 125
Boyd, Alan S., 212
Brantley, 213
Brelsford, J. B., 26
Brequet, Louis, 20, 22, 30, 32, 33
Brie, R. A. C., 84, 125
Buckley, Clifford, 179
Burleigh, Manferd, 157
Burleigh, Mrs. Manferd, 157
Byrd, Richard E., 160

Caesar, Orville S., 157
Calloway, A. Gordon, 76
Carlson, Floyd, 151
Carroll Franklin O., 26, 29, 75, 76, 77, 85, 92, 101
Carroll, Mrs. Franklin O. (Clara), 77

Carter, W. C., 66
Cayley, Sir George, 20
Chalker, L. T., 66
Chandler, Rex E., 76
Chanute, Octave, 21
Chidlaw, Ben W., 66, 76, 125, 127, 133, 139
Clingler, Leo M., 60, 62
Cochran, Phil, 204
Conner, R. P., 59
Cooper, Leslie B., 84, 92, 103, 115, 116, 123, 125, 128, 129, 131, 132
Cornu, Paul, 21, 22
Counter, H. M., 132
Courtoy, Colette, 165
Courtoy, Marcel, 163, 164
Courtoy, Marcel, Jr., 165
Courtoy, Monique, 165
Courtoy, Mrs. Marcel, 165
Courtoy, Suzanne, 165
Craigie, L. C. "Bill", 77, 92, 133, 139
Crittenberger, W. D., 66
Crocker, Francis B., 32
Crowley, John W. "Gus", 66, 76
Curtiss, Glen, 21, 40
Czar of Russia, 22

Daland, Elliott, 150
Damblanc, Louis, 33
d'Ascanio, Coradino, 33, 68
da Vinci, Leonardo, 19
deBothezat, George, 23, 24, 25, 26, 27, 28, 30, 31, 67, 75, 145
de la Cierva, Juan, 34, 35
Delear, Frank J., 11, 13
Denny, Corwin, 150
Dixon, Jess, 154
Doolittle, James H., 104
Dorsey, Frank J. G., 64
Douheret, 23
Dvergnes, Anstein, 199

Easton, John, 66
Echols, Oliver P., 76, 133
Edgerton, J. C., 115
Edison, Thomas A., 20, 21

Ellahammer, 33
Erickson, Frank, 125, 155, 199
Erickson, Jack, 186

Fales, E. W., 66
Felt, Jack D., 60
Fleming, Morton D., 142
Flettner, 60
Florine, Nicolas, 33, 35
Focke, 51, 60, 64
Ford, Henry, 32
Forlanini, Enrico, 20
Franklin, John W., 113, 124, 125
Franks, Robert G., 60, 62
Frohlich, Ed, 118

Gabel, P. Ernest, 60, 62, 84, 103
Gafney, Dale F., 131
Gerhardt, W. F., 30
Gillet, Charles, 163, 164
Gluhareff, Michael, 73
Gluhareff, Serge, 75, 87, 139
Greene, Carl F., 73, 74
Gregory, Mrs. H. Franklin (Betty), 157
Grewell, O. D., 26
Griggs, David T. 125
Godwin, J. P., 66
Gough, Mel, 40, 42, 43, 45, 46
Guggenhein, 63

Hafner, Raoul, 35
Hagemeyer, Louis, 125
Hamilton, Donald, 76
Harman, Carter, 199
Harris, H. R., 30
Haugen, Victor R., 66, 74, 75, 76
Haynes, Baylor, 174
Helber, C. L., 66
Helds, C. S., 66
Hermes, Harold H., 125, 128
Hewitt, Peter Cooper, 24, 32, 33
Higgins, 148, 150
Hill, Arthur M., 157
Hiller, Stanley, 213
Hladkovkak, Ernest, 199
Holder, J. H., 124, 125